CONSISTENCY IS KEY

JAY JOHNSON

CONSISTENCY IS KEY

15 Ways to Unlock Your Potential as a High School Runner

To inquire about special discounts or bulk orders, please visit
PFBpublishing.com or email info@PFBpublishing.com

Published by PFB Publishing, LLC, 2020
Printed in the United States of America

Library of Congress Cataloging-in-Publication Data
Name: Johnson, Jay J., author.
Title: Consistency is key : 15 ways to unlock your potential as a high school runner / Jay Johnson.
Description: First Edition | Denver, CO: PFB Publishing, LLC, 2020.
Identifiers: LCCN: 2020908475 | ISBN: 978-0-578-68504-5
Subjects: LCSH Running. | Track and field. | Track and field--Athletes. | School sports.
Classification: LCC GV1060.5.J64 2020 | DDC 796.4/2--dc23

Edited by Kyle Wyatt
Cover and interior pages designed by Adam Batliner
Illustrations copyright © 2020 Adam Batliner

DISCLAIMER
This book is for informational and educational purposes. Please consult your health care provider before beginning any exercise program.

This book is dedicated to my daughters,
Lulu and Avery.

You remind me daily that reading is a joy.

This book is for you, a high school runner.

Preface

In the early 1990s, I was a decent, but not exceptional, high school runner in Castle Rock, Colorado. I had a number of minor successes, the biggest being that I ran just fast enough my senior year to walk on at the University of Colorado.

For several years in Boulder, I was the slowest varsity guy on some very good cross country teams. In 1998, my senior year, I was part of the squad that finished third at the NCAA Cross Country Championships, but I wasn't a scorer. There is a book about that season of ours, *Running with the Buffaloes*, and maybe you'll read it someday when you're in college. It contains a number of great lessons, but what works in the NCAA doesn't always translate to high school racing and training.

There is a lesson that's universal, though: the gift of confidence. No matter a runner's ability—whether they've just barely made varsity or they're about to defend their state title—any runner can step onto the starting line ready to execute a race plan with confidence.

This book is about gifting yourself with that confidence. Besides *Running with the Buffaloes*, there are many inspiring books about our sport, from novels like *Once a Runner* to nonfiction works about Emil Zatopek and Deena Kastor. But most of these books focus on older athletes running longer races. Again, the great lessons don't always translate for teenagers. This book, however, is for you—a high school runner.

This book makes some assumptions about you:

1. It assumes you want to have fun.

2. It assumes you want to compete—against yourself and against your competitors.

3. It assumes you want to have a lot of fun in those competitions.

4. It assumes you want to see how fast you can run.

5. It assumes you value track and field as much as you do cross country.

You might relate to some of the assumptions on the opposite page more than others, and that's okay. Some runners thrive in major competitions, and others just like to race the clock. Same with liking cross country and disliking track: it's okay to prefer one over the other, and preferring the one you're better at is completely understandable. The very best runners, though, value both seasons. They see the connection between the two, just like they see the connection between having fun and competing well.

I sometimes lost sight of the fun when I ran in high school, because I was constantly questioning my team's training. Were we just winging it, I often wondered. When I arrived at CU, I followed the training to the letter my first two years, and I made a huge jump compared to my high school times. As a college sophomore, for instance, I came through the 3,200m mark of a 5,000m race some 30 seconds faster than my high school 3,200m PR and then sped up over the remaining four and a half laps.

But as a junior, I added unauthorized double runs and weightlifting in my training, in hopes of improving. My self-directed experiment led to a year and a half of poor training and pitiful racing. I simply dug a hole and struggled to get out. There was a silver lining to this period, though: As I became more and more curious about human physiology, and how our bodies and minds can best work together, I decided to become a coach. I was on track to get my undergraduate degree in kinesiology, and I decided to pursue a master's degree in it and applied physiology, which gave me the background to understand the exercise physiology that informs the 15 lessons of this book.

After hanging up my spikes, I didn't leave the sport. Instead, I began my coaching career, nearly 20 years ago, at Pratt Community College in Kansas. A few years later, I headed back to CU. After that, I had the chance to coach several professional runners, three of whom won USATF championships. Along the way, I have continued to learn about physiology, training philosophies, and race strategies—their differences and their similarities. But perhaps best of all, I have worked with high school athletes since 2003 as the director of the Boulder Running Camps. It's this rewarding experience that has truly shaped the book that follows.

I have many opinions on training, racing, and how coaches can work to build a culture where running is fun—where working to become faster is a joyful process. This is not a book full of my opinions, though. Rather, it explains the fundamentals of running—fundamentals that all good coaches will agree on. Here's an example: It's not my opinion that a block of injury-free training, with thoughtful workouts and adequate recovery, will almost always lead to good performances. Coaches at every level, and successful runners who have been running for years, will agree with this fundamental truth. It's also not my opinion that the well-rested athlete will be able to train and race at higher levels than an athlete who fails to get adequate sleep. It's not my opinion that training the aerobic system must be done every month of the year if an athlete is to reach his or her potential. And it's not my opinion that if the word "consistent" can honestly describe your training, you will find yourself racing at or near your potential.

So, are you ready to get started?

Ready
to get
started?

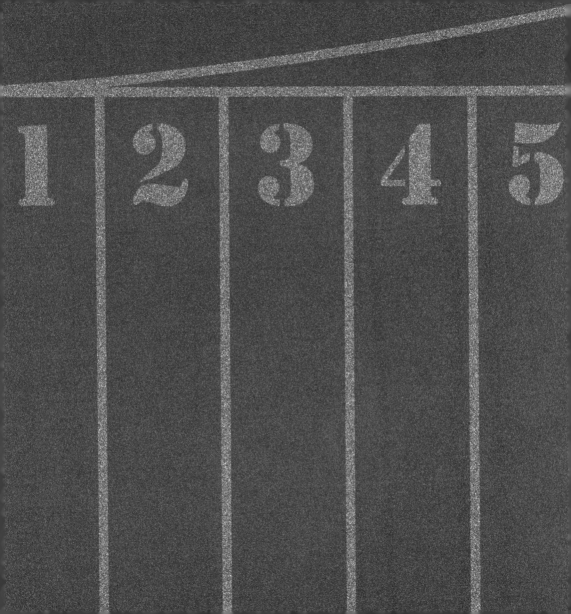

Introduction

This book is a resource that I wish I could have read in high school. I wrote it to be fun the first time through, and to be a helpful resource if you flip through it a second or third time. I tried to fill it with information that isn't going to change in the coming decades. Shoes will improve, track surfaces will improve, and the technology used to make your uniform will improve, but the importance of consistency in training will not change.

This book is for you. It's not for your coach, your parents, or your neighbor who runs marathons and likes to give you pointers. I hope your coach will find this book useful, and that he or she agrees with its major themes. If your parents want to understand our sport on a deeper level, they may find these pages useful too. Yet, ultimately, this is a resource for the high school runner— whether a new runner who has just joined the cross country or track team or a more seasoned one who is dying to race faster and is hungry for information on how to do so.

Most high school runners assume that if they simply run more miles and train harder, they will run faster. And that is true to a point. What few high school runners know when they first join the cross country or track team is that consistency is the key to long-term improvement. In this book, we'll talk about workouts, we'll talk about running more miles and running some of those miles harder, and we'll talk about all of the non-running exercises you need to do to stay injury-free. But before we go into those topics, you need to internalize one thing above all else: if your goal is to run progressively faster at the end of each season, then consistency is the key.

If a high school runner trains 48 weeks a year and trains six days a week, the chances of improving from season to season are extremely high. It's also okay to run just four or five days a week in some circumstances, especially if you're just starting. If you're new to running, you'll gain fitness quickly. If you've been running for several years, you won't gain fitness as dramatically, but you'll still gain it month to month, season to season, and year to year—as long as you stay injury-free and have fun. If you're a student of the sport and love learning about the training of collegiate and professional athletes, that's great. Yet know those athletes require a level of sophistication that you do not need to improve yourself. If you stay healthy, commit to training 48 weeks a year, and train six days a week, you'll have what you need for success. Later in the book, we will discuss programs where some older athletes run more than the 288 days each year that I just described. If you trust that consistency is the key to

If your goal is to run progressively faster at the end of each season, then consistency is the key.

improvement, the question is, What are the other key elements I need to get fit and race fast?

The following four factors impact training and are covered in the first portion of most running books. I want to acknowledge their importance before we move along:

1. **Volume.** This simply means how much you're running. You can measure this in miles or minutes or a combination of both (which is what many great high school programs do).

2. **Intensity.** How hard (or easy) you approach a run, a workout, or a race.

3. **Non-Running Work.** You've likely heard of core strength, which is a classic example. We'll discuss all the additional exercises and routines you could incorporate to stay injury-free. Videos are a great way to learn this work, and I'll share online resources later in the book.

4. **Recovery.** The harder your workout or race, the more recovery you need. This changes a bit as you get older and can handle more training.

Each of these four factors matter; you simply can't improve without them. But now that we've acknowledged their importance, I'd like you to begin considering what else it'll take for your long-term success in the sport.

Ideally, you'll make lots of small, incremental improvements over many weeks, months, seasons, and years. This means that if your long run is an hour today, you shouldn't try to run for 75 minutes next week or 90 minutes the week after that. Yes, training volume relates to racing faster, and a longer long run usually (but not always) translates to faster races. Jumping from an hour-long run to a 90-minute one in a couple weeks' time might be tempting, especially when you're feeling good. But it is simply too big a jump in too little time. For many runners, the motivation to improve needs to be held in check by coaches and teammates. Their long-run progression, like all other aspects of their training and racing, needs to be consistent.

In this book, you'll learn about 15 ways to unlock your potential. I've grouped these points into four sections. Before you even lace up your shoes, you need to understand that talent and excellence are not the same thing. But there's good news in that! I'll show in the first section how you can build your attention span for hard work and become an excellent runner, even if you're not the most "naturally talented" athlete on your team. It's important to understand that your progress will not be linear, even if your effort and commitment to excellence is consistent. And before we talk about training, know that there are dozens of solid approaches. You simply need a training plan that has proven fundamentals at its core (even if your team's plan looks a little different than a rival's).

The next section covers what you'll need to train, and that's pretty simple. Using the analogy of a car, I'll explain why you need to build your aerobic engine and why you need to strengthen your chassis. You also need to rev that engine most days with strides—an element that is crucial to your development. From there, I'll explain how to train, along with the importance of running by feel. You need your easy days to be easy, so that your hard days can be hard. This combination sets you up for the race-pace workouts that are essential for realizing your potential. The last two concepts you need to embrace are simple but not easy to execute. For challenging runs, when you finish you need to be able to say that you could have gone farther or faster (or both). When you do challenging workouts, in both cross country and track, "fast, faster, fastest" applies in two ways. You want the last three repetitions to be fast, faster and fastest. And you want to be able to change gears within the last rep or two, mimicking what you'll have to do in a race.

You'll need to support your training with solid sleep and nutrition, and in the third section, I'll offer reasonable suggestions that you can implement (and trust me, I know the stressors in your life are numerous and significant). Learning to listen to your body is a skill that you can cultivate throughout your high school career, and through these pages and the videos that accompany this book, you'll learn self-care techniques that can help you stay injury-free.

Finally, we'll revisit the idea that there are dozens of ways to train. I'll give examples of how some of the best programs in the country use fundamental principles, which your own team might arrange in different ways. No two programs build the aerobic engine the same way, for example, yet athletes in these programs all race fast. You'll read about teams that have great depth, meaning athletes of many abilities improve together throughout the year. I'll share these examples not so you can piece together a new training system—taking elements from each program—but rather to solidify the concept that there are dozens of ways to train.

There are dozens of ways to train.

"When you have the enthusiasm and the passion, you end up figuring how to excel."

—DEENA KASTOR

Before You Even Lace Up Your Shoes

1. Remember That Talent and Excellence Are Not the Same Thing

To become a better runner in the coming months and years, you'll have to train with good energy and focus, and you'll have to train intelligently. Do that, and you'll improve. Do that, and you'll soon be ready to race faster. I like to call this "transcending a former self." Your friends who play ball sports don't have the same objective results that you have as a distance runner. A girl who runs 5:30 for the 1,600m as a sophomore transcends her former self when she runs 5:20 as a junior. How cool is that?

So training hard, training smart, and focusing on staying healthy will allow you to make a jump in fitness and race faster. That said, genetic talent plays a role in distance running. Let's consider two hypothetical athletes: James and Daniel.

As eighth graders, James and Daniel both played soccer in the fall, basketball in the winter, and ran track in the spring, training four or five days a week. Plus, the season was only eight weeks long. The point is that James and Daniel had

If you train intelligently with good energy and focus, you'll soon be ready to race faster.

virtually identical athletic backgrounds in middle school.

The summer before high school, James and Daniel decide to go out for cross country, and that fall they both run in the low 18:00 range for the 5,000m. They do almost identical training over the winter, and are both excited for their first high school track season. But then their performances start to diverge: Daniel starts to race faster than James.

Daniel runs a 4:50 1,600m in the third meet of the year, while James runs a very respectable 5:00 in the same race. Two weeks later, they race their first 3,200m. Daniel runs 10:18, while James runs 10:39. The following week, at a small dual meet, they both run the 800m. Daniel runs a solid 2:12, while James runs a decent but not stellar 2:16.

Again, Daniel and James did the same sports in middle school, and they have done almost identical training thus far in high school. Daniel is no more serious than James: They both love the sport and are dying to race faster. They do the same workouts and runs, too. Yet Daniel is simply faster than James.

I'd like you to understand two things from this hypothetical example.

The first is that Daniel simply has more genetic talent than James. Does that mean James should quit running and do something else? Absolutely not. Remember, they both love the sport and are dying to race faster. There is no reason James shouldn't continue to train with enthusiasm, even if his PRs aren't as fast as Daniel's.

Second, while you can't control the genetic talent you're born with, you can focus on becoming the best runner you can be. The journey of transcending a former self throughout your high school career is an experience that you don't want to miss. I see this every year at my running camps: The girls in the top group aren't more focused than the girls in the second or third groups. The girls in the top group simply have more talent. Each year I am reminded of the dedication of the girls in the second and third groups, who have just as much fun and are just as invested in the journey of becoming the best high school runners they can be.

The chance to ride the bus to meets, to dress up for Halloween during cross country season, to do a killer workout in the rain with your friends—these are all experiences you can have in high school, but not as an adult runner. You don't need to have exceptional talent to chase excellence! What's more, you can have an exceptional experience running in high school with the exact amount of talent you have. The flip side is this: your experience as a high school athlete won't be as rich and meaningful as it can be if you aren't working a bit harder each season.

*While you can't control the genetic talent you're born with, you can focus on becoming the best runner **you** can be.*

22

2. Build Your Attention Span for Hard Work

Whether or not you're the most talented athlete on your team, you want to have an exceptional experience running in high school. To do this, you need to build your attention span for hard work.

Consider the term "long run." This is the most time you'll spend on your feet each week, and it will last much longer than a race. Staying engaged mentally, making sure you're running with great posture from start to finish, and making sure the pace doesn't slow down toward the end—these all build your attention span for hard work. After you have a few long runs under your belt, you can either increase the distance or increase the pace of the run. (Later on, I'll explain why increasing the pace is often a better choice.)

As a high school athlete, you're obviously going to train fewer minutes or miles per week than professional athletes, yet the non-running work you need to be doing after each run or workout might be as challenging and lengthy as theirs. It's not uncommon for a determined high school athlete to do 20 minutes of non-running work following every run, and as much as 30 minutes a couple of times a week on the harder days. Strength and mobility exercises can be simple, but they're not easy. A determined athlete can hold a plank for 10 seconds, regardless of how hard he or she ran during a workout. And a 10-second plank can soon become a 15-second one, which is a great indicator that you're slowly getting stronger, even if you're unable to run more minutes or miles. You just have to build the attention span to improve your planks.

Here's the deal: You can't change who your parents are. You can't change the genetic talent you were born with. But you can change your capacity for hard work. Staying engaged mentally on a long run, making the last 10 to 20 minutes the best minutes of the run, or doing challenging non-running work following a challenging workout are all examples. My favorite quote for runners is from the iconic jazz pianist Thelonious Monk: "Simple ain't easy." I'm not saying running hard long runs and doing 15, 20, or even 30 minutes of non-running work is going to be easy, but it's definitely not complex. If Thelonious Monk had been a runner, he might have said, "Running is simple, but it's not easy."

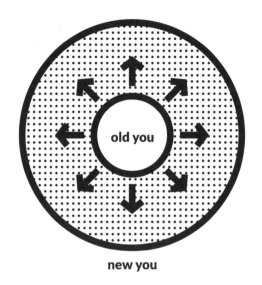

old you

new you

You can change your capacity for hard work.

3. Know That Progress Is Not Linear

You might reasonably assume that you'll race faster month after month if you stay injury-free and do the training that you and your coach believe is best. Unfortunately, this type of linear improvement isn't the reality for a high school athlete, nor is it true for collegiate and professional athletes. Here are a couple of reasons why.

Let's say an athlete chooses to train the summer before her freshman year of high school and continues running through outdoor track her senior year. That gives her four distinct windows of opportunity to improve each year: summer training, cross country, winter training, and outdoor track. In total, she'll have 16 chances to improve during high school, yet if you graphed her improvement, you would not see a perfectly straight line. If she falls in love with the sport during freshman cross country, she may be extremely motivated to train that following winter. The fitness she gains will, with intelligent training, lead to fast racing in outdoor track. That track season, she'll have "made a jump."

Let's say this same girl is unable to train as well the following summer. Her family vacation and her summer job end up being more demanding than she anticipated. She's still running, and she's still gaining fitness—just not as dramatically as she did the previous season. Once school starts and she can get into a routine—balancing school, running, family, and a social life—she will no doubt see improvements. But, again, they may not be as dramatic as before. And you know what? That's okay!

There's another reason your progress won't be as linear as you might like. Most committed high school runners will experience some minor setback once or twice a calendar year—a little niggle that requires them to take a day or two off or cross train for a few days.

Many runners use the word "niggle" to describe little issues, usually soft tissue in nature that with the right treatment cause only a minor interruption in training (think a tight hamstring or sore Achilles, but not something bone related). More serious than a niggle is an injury. Some coaches tell athletes that injuries are, unfortunately, part of the sport. This is absolutely true for professionals, but I do not want you to embrace this mentality as a high school runner. I'd encourage you and your coach to have this mentality instead: "We control so many of the variables that could lead to an injury, and we're both going to do our part to stay injury-free."

For your coach, this means writing sound progressions for everything you do: running volume, running intensity, non-running work, and so on. Your coach

The annoying reality is that you may plateau on occasion.

even needs a progression for racing shoes, because so often a lower-leg niggle or injury comes from racing in spikes when you've only done strides in them—without actually having put them to the test in a workout.

Remember when I said that this is not a book of opinions? Well, some veteran coaches may disagree with my views on injuries. Let me be clear: I believe it's realistic that a committed athlete can run four years in high school and never miss more than a small number of days due to niggles. We've established that consistency is the key for long-term success; staying mostly injury-free leads to consistent training, which leads to faster racing. This requires thoughtful, skillful planning on your coach's part, and a commitment to excellence on yours. As long as both of you do your part, you should be able to train injury-free (though not necessarily niggle-free).

Later in the book, I'll share some ideas about how to listen to your body, specifically learning the skill of differentiating between the minor muscle soreness and general fatigue that is part of training and the more serious pain that needs to be addressed in different ways. What's great about this era of running is that there are numerous ways to stay injury-free with the help of self-therapy. The determined high school athlete can make the time for preventative maintenance work throughout the week.

So what happens if you do experience more than a niggle? What about big injuries, like a stress fracture, that keep you from running for several weeks? "Simple ain't easy" still applies. You can keep three basic concepts in mind: First, follow the directions of the medical professionals helping you. Second, do all of the training you're cleared to do. For instance, if you have a stress reaction in your shin (tibia), you can still swim or pool run quite a bit. And you'll get a prescription of general strength and mobility work that you can do as well. Third, and often the most challenging, keep a calm mind and remind yourself that too much frustration (or anger or sadness or anxiety) can actually increase recovery time. You have to find ways to stay calm-minded, and you need to view this period as relatively short when you consider the length of a high school running career—a career that may even lead to collegiate running.

Whether it is a niggle, an injury, or a family vacation that keeps you from training at 100 percent, the annoying reality is that you may plateau on occasion. Don't panic! Every seasoned runner at every level deals with this. Even with a conservative approach to training, and under the guidance of a veteran coach who is exceptional at his or her craft, an athlete who is determined to improve will not be able to train at 100 percent every day of every year.

32

4. Understand That There Are Dozens Of Ways To Train

In the next two sections, we're going to talk about training—what to train and how to train it. But before we dive into the nuts and bolts, we need to establish an important concept: there are dozens of ways to train on your journey to becoming an exceptional high school runner.

Over the past several years, I've had the chance to learn from some of the best high school coaches in the country. In talking with them and watching their athletes, I've gained insight into how they design and implement their programs. I've had the chance to study their workouts, and have interviewed many of them. I'm always wondering, Why do these successful coaches do what they do? The answers are fascinating (at least for a running geek like me).

At the end of the day, there are successful programs at small schools and big schools, and at every size in between. It doesn't matter if the adjective "rural," "suburban," or "urban" applies to a school: it can still have an amazing program filled with exceptional high school runners. Some programs have a separate coach for girls and boys, while other schools have a single coach for both teams.

There are no magic workouts.

Over the years, I have identified some consistent ingredients that character-ize ultra-successful programs—teams that are competitive at both the state and national levels. Not every school uses all of these ingredients, and few programs put them together in exactly the same way. And that means you and your coach can incorporate these elements of success in ways that make sense for you, your team, and your environment—and can set you up to excel season after season.

None of the programs I have studied do identical workouts, for one thing, and each coach structures their athletes' training weeks differently. Some pro-grams make the long run a weekly cornerstone, while others do them infre-quently. Simply put, there are no magic workouts. Some programs go to the weight room three times a week, and others go once or twice a week. And, yes, some teams never hit the weight room. Yet all are successful.

For generations, runners have kept training logs, and several programs make this storied practice a key element. Other programs have coaches who essentially keep a mental log of workouts and the overall training load. Most successful coaches know that specific workouts or training approaches don't matter as much as their athletes might guess. But they agree that building an athlete's attention span for hard work is essential. They know that successful runners rarely progress in a linear fashion—whether week over week, month over month, or even season over season. Your willingness to be okay with that—that your own progress may *not* be linear—is crucial. This is a sport that asks you to stay focused not only in workouts and races, but also for months and years at a time. Ideally, you will slowly fall in love with the process of being a runner—a process of small choices made day after day, and week after week—to see how fast you can run, regardless of your genetic talent.

It's up to you and your coach to come up with a training recipe that's specific to your environment and your school. Think about it: the runner who lives in a rural town with miles of hilly dirt roads will inevitably do things differently than a runner who lives in a dense urban area that is pancake flat and has lots of stoplights. Trust your coach to formulate a plan that's a great fit for you and your team. And then get to work.

"*Everything should be made as simple as possible, but not simpler.*"

—ALBERT EINSTEIN

What to Train

5. Build Your Aerobic Engine

Think of your body as a car. While the analogy isn't perfect, it can help you understand some of the keys to consistent improvement.

Distance runners need to build their aerobic engines if they want to race faster. And the reason is simple: what's known as your aerobic metabolism contributes the majority of the energy that your muscles need to power you down the track or around the cross country course.

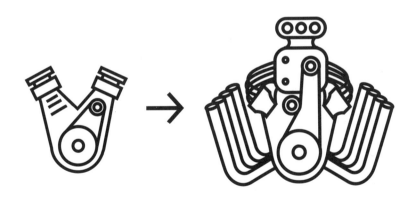

Take a moment to consider the following table:

Distance	Aerobic %	Anaerobic %	Phosphogen %
800m	60%	35%	5%
1,600m	82%*	18%	0–2%
3,200m	90%	10%	0–2%
5,000m	95%	5%	0–2%

*There is a debate as to the exact percentage for the 1,600m, ranging from 80% to 85%

There's a lot going on in this table, but you really only need to take away two essential points. First, every distance you'll race is more aerobic than anaerobic—in other words, the energy system that requires oxygen is doing more of the work than the energy systems that don't. Second, the aerobic contributions to performance increase as the distance gets longer (with a 5,000m cross country race being 95 percent aerobic).

It's these two points that shape effective training programs for distance runners: you need to focus on building your aerobic engine throughout the year because races ranging from 1,600m to 5,000m are primarily powered aerobically.

Put another way, if you do the right aerobic workouts, you can transform a four-cylinder engine into a V-6.

Distance runners need to build their aerobic engines if they want to race faster.

Beyond the car analogy, it's worth knowing a little more about the terms "aerobic" and "anaerobic." The most basic definitions are "with oxygen" and "without oxygen," respectively. Once you gain some level of fitness, you can hold a conversation while running at a steady pace, whereas before maybe you could only manage a few words here and there. This difference in fitness points to where you're getting your energy—increasingly via aerobic metabolism.

Now picture running 200m as fast as you can. Your body has different types of muscles, and you use both your fast-twitch muscles and your slow-twitch muscles to run all out. Your fast-twitch muscles are special, in that they can produce a lot of force without oxygen. But however powerful, they need a bit of help from their slow-twitch counterparts.

Take another moment and think about how you feel when you're barreling down the track for 200m. Can you feel a burning sensation in your chest or in your legs? Maybe a metallic taste in your mouth? That's because your body is producing lactate, a byproduct of those fast-twitch muscles at work— muscles that weren't using oxygen. So they're special muscles, yes, but there's a tradeoff when you put them to work!

At this point, most running books would include several pages about exercise physiology—going into detail about lactate production and the associated H+ ions, and how the body can buffer these ions while keeping blood pH from dropping dramatically. (If you want to learn more about the science of running, I have plenty of resources for you at CoachJayJohnson.com/CIKbook.) But to be an excellent high school runner, you only need to know the two key points I mentioned above, and to trust that your aerobic training is supported by science.

To build your aerobic engine, you need to do the correct types of workouts that enhance this system. Later in the book, in "How to Train," I'll explain why long runs, fartlek runs, progression runs, and threshold runs are four great options (but by no means are they the only options). Each of these teach you to run by feel, which is a crucial part of becoming a better runner. Running by feel, as compared to training at a predetermined pace, allows you to execute a workout as it was intended. Plus, it prevents you from overextending yourself, which can start a cascade of overly hard training days that lead to deep fatigue and possibly injury. But first, let's talk about the structure that holds your aerobic engine—your chassis.

44

6. Strengthen Your Chassis

A car's chassis is the frame that holds the engine, as well as the other machinery that makes it move. Using a car analogy, your bones are your body's main structure, and your muscles and tendons, as well as your ligaments and fascia, also form part of your chassis. Strengthening each of these is crucial to staying injury-free. If you can stay injury-free, having to miss only a day or two here and there with a niggle, you're going to race faster.

This is also important, but not always understood by athletes and coaches: young athletes can "build their engines" faster than they can build their chassis. My friend Mike Smith, who coached at Kansas State University, introduced me to this concept when I was coaching at the University of Colorado. "Metabolic changes occur faster than structural changes," he explained. And that's why he had his college athletes do so much work to strengthen all the components of their chassis. For high school athletes, who are often coming into running with modest athletic backgrounds, engines can improve dramatically in just a few months. That means they need to spend a significant amount of time strength training, so that both their engines and chassis improve at roughly the same rate.

What do you need to do to strengthen your chassis? Two things, one of which might not be obvious.

First, you need to do some sort of strength and mobility work every day that you run (I'll often refer to this type of work as SAM, short for "strength and mobility"). You need more than stronger muscles; you also need good mobility, specifically at the hip joint, a problem area for many runners. Another problem for many runners, even professionals, is a weak back of the body, what we call the "posterior chain." When runners strengthen their posterior chain—think low back, glutes, and hamstrings—they decrease their chances of injury, while developing their capacity to sprint faster and run fast paces for longer periods of time.

If you want to be the best runner possible, then take 10 minutes to watch some of the videos I've prepared around SAM exercises and routines. Go to my website to get a feel for this essential work. Once you've done that, you need to do something else—something simple yet extremely difficult for most runners. And that is the second part of the "strengthen your chassis" equation.

Put simply: you must value your non-running training, such as strength and mobility work, as much as you value your running. Will you spend more time running than you'll spend doing SAM work? Absolutely. And will you be more excited to do long runs and workouts, as well as easy runs, than you'll be excited to do SAM exercises? Yes. But to stay injury-free and to have consistency define your training, please value strength and mobility work just

When you strengthen your chassis, you set yourself up to safely run more.

as much as you value getting out the door to run. Here's the real beauty of this equation: when you strengthen your chassis, you set yourself up to *safely* run more miles or minutes and to *safely* run more intense runs or workouts. If you're dying to race faster, if you want to run more, or if you want to train at greater intensities, SAM work will help get you there.

It's also worth noting that there are a lot of good exercises that don't fall under the strict category of "strength and mobility." You may have already spent time in the weight room to strength train with your cross country or track team, or with another sport. If you have been in the weight room, I hope your coaches shared with you an important concept. Even if they have, it's worth repeating here: strength training should progress from body weight to light external loads to heavy external loads, and it should progress over the course of months and years, not days and weeks.

Body Weight ➞ Light External Load ➞ Heavy External Load

The SAM routine videos I mentioned above are all examples of body weight exercises that will help you, over time, gain a great deal of muscular strength. Once you have it, you can move into some light external loads. Grabbing a medicine ball and then doing a circuit with a teammate is an example of this type of work. Heavy external load exercises typically involve the weight room. Under the guidance of a skilled coach, you can safely lift weights in ways that complement your running.

But also know this: going to the weight room is not necessary to be an excellent high school runner. When I was a young college coach, I learned the "weight room without walls" concept, developed by Vern Gambetta, a strength coach whose roots are in track and field. I loved this concept because it reminded me that medicine balls, hurdles, and mini-bands—all relatively affordable training tools that you can use at the track or after an easy run—allow you to accomplish a variety of strength training almost anywhere. To do this work at home, you only need to make a modest investment of time and money. You'll need to buy a medicine ball and some mini-bands, and eventually a kettlebell, then spend an afternoon building hurdles out of PVC pipes (which is easier than it sounds).

After years of coaching, I've come to see Coach Smith's "metabolic changes occur faster than structural changes" observation just a bit differently. In my mind, and with my athletes, I switch the wording to "structural changes take longer than metabolic changes." Why? This perspective emphasizes patience. You don't need to be excited to do the non-running work, but you need to value it as much as you do your runs and workouts.

With a modest investment of time and money, you can strength train almost anywhere.

7. Rev the Engine Most Days

Staying with the car analogy, it's important that you "rev the engine" most days by doing strides. A stride is simply a quick, short sprint—anywhere between 70m and 150m—that's faster than your race pace and much faster than your training paces. The principle of revving the engine most days applies to runners specializing in multiple distances: high school cross country runners need to incorporate strides that are faster than 5,000m pace throughout the year. So, too, do 800m runners, who need to run significantly faster than race pace to reach their full potential in their chosen event. And no matter an athlete's preferred distance, he or she needs to go fast whether in season or not.

When I talk to high school athletes about training, and we look for places where they can make simple adjustments right away, I find it's this revving the engine concept that's most often missing. While many athletes do strides one or two days a week during their season, they aren't doing them most days that they run. You need to incorporate strides if you want to race to your potential. There are two simple reasons: You have to practice running faster than race pace to internalize that "challenging but doable" effort so it feels realistic when the gun goes off. And you must regularly rehearse speeding up—or "changing gears"—if you want to do the same thing in a race.

Athletes typically have one of several problems with strides. First, they don't do them the first day of summer training. Instead, they wait a week or two, and then add them to the mix. Second, if they do strides the first day of summer training, they don't have a progression in mind. For example, in three weeks' time, do you run more strides, do you run longer strides, do you run faster strides, or do you do some combination of these three variables? The key is to plan out a progression for revving your engine. Third, some athletes are afraid that if they run fast in the summer (or in the winter, as they prepare for outdoor track), they'll "peak" too early.

Let's assume that the first day of summer practice starts in early or mid-June. Now fast-forward to mid- to late-September, and envision the type of cross country race you may want to execute. While your coach will have a slightly different game plan for each course you run, many courses lend themselves to a similar approach: It will be important to start a bit faster than intended race pace the first 100m or 200m, to secure a good position, and then run a challenging pace until the 4,000m or 4,400m mark. You and your coach may decide that, with 600m to go, you should speed up for 400m before running the final 200m to the finish as hard as you can. With this type of plan, you will likely run four paces: the faster pace in the opening 100m to 200m, the challenging but realistic pace for the majority of distance, faster for 400m, and finally your fastest over the last 200m.

Here's the deal: if you haven't done strides in the months leading up to this hypothetical September race, you'll struggle to execute your plan. If the fastest running you've done in the summer is 1,600m pace, more or less, then the first 100m to 200m on the cross country course will seem too fast. Such a perception can shake the confidence of even the most seasoned upperclassmen! In those first few seconds after the gun goes off, there is a good chance everyone will be running faster than 1,600m pace. You don't want the start to feel chaotic or beyond your abilities, so you should make sure you've run these paces in June, July, and August.

The middle of the race should feel challenging, because your engine is working as hard as it can to maintain race pace for roughly 4,400m. Of course, you don't want that "challenging but doable" pace to feel too fast. Consistently doing strides throughout the summer will ensure that the majority of the race doesn't feel too fast, which, in turn, will help you compete with a calm mind. When it comes time to speed up over the last 600m or so, your body needs to know what to do: how to run even faster on legs that aren't 100 percent. Finally, to cover the last 200m race the fastest you can—especially considering you've already been running hard for almost three miles—you need to have done dozens and dozens of strides over several months.

If you agree that summertime strides are important, then the question is when should you do them? Do you run them every day? Do you run them at the beginning of practice, when your legs are fresh, or do you conclude practice with them, when you're a bit tired? What's the best surface to run them on, especially if you have the luxury of having both a flat, safe grass field and a relatively soft track? What if you find yourself without a stretch of safe footing for strides? All great questions.

First, when should you rev your engine during practice? At the beginning of a session, you should do some muscle activation and dynamic warm-up exercises. At the end of practice, you should finish with some sort of strength and mobility work. If you're doing an easy run, your strides can come at the end—that's typically what most programs do. In this scenario, I like to see athletes go immediately into their strides to keep their heart rate elevated, which adds to the engine building for the day. There's one problem with scheduling strides at the end of the run: it's easy to finish your daily miles and lack the motivation to complete your strides, even though you know they're a crucial part of intelligent training.

My personal preference is that you run your strides as part of your easy run, as this ensures they get done. You simply run them in the last 30 to 40 percent of your prescribed distance or duration. If your coach assigns you a 50-minute run, for example, with 5 x 20 seconds at 3,200m effort, then you can start your

strides roughly 35 minutes into the run. Even if you take as much easy running in between the strides as you need, this little assignment will take more than 5 minutes but less than 10. And then you simply resume your easy pace until you reach the 50-minute mark.

Coaches and athletes tell me they really like this approach for two reasons. First, it ensures that the strides get done. Second, if the athlete is focused on doing them with good posture, this approach can indicate that he or she did, in fact, do the easy run at a comfortable pace, and that he or she is recovering properly from the past few days of training. In other words, strides done in the last third of a run offer a glimpse into how an athlete is handling his or her overall training load. A tired athlete will have trouble running strides at the end of a run—even an easy one—if the overall workload is too challenging.

It's important to understand the progression of strides from the first day of summer training to the start of the cross country season, and from the start of winter training to the start of outdoor track. For an example of what that progression might look like, visit CoachJayJohnson.com/CIKbook and find a plan that has the effort level, distance, and number of strides you can consider doing in the summer and winter months. Obviously, these are just guidelines, and your coach may have a different progression that he or she wants you to follow. The same thing goes with the surface you'll run the strides on: let your coach guide this aspect of training. Most coaches will have a variety of surfaces to choose from, and they will factor this aspect of strides into the progression. And if you're away from your normal training routes, because you're on summer vacation, for example, be mindful of safe surfaces. While strides are great, they're not worth doing if the footing is too uneven or too slippery.

Many athletes will ask, "Will I peak too early if I'm doing strides the first week of practice in the summer?" Not at all. No athlete wants to run his or her best races of the season in September, then perform a bit worse with each successive race in October. That would mean the peak came in September. While coaches love to debate the concept of peaking (I personally don't like using it), there is no doubt that we want to ensure that your best racing comes in the championship season, which is in October and November in most states. A year-long commitment to running strides most days will have your legs ready to run some race-pace workouts in August. You need to do those workouts to run well in September, and solid races in September lead to fast racing in October. I'm not suggesting workouts at race pace in the summer, but I am suggesting that for short distances—70m to 150m—you should run fast so that when the time comes to run race pace, that rhythm will feel comfortable.

"All athletes who strive for excellence share the same story."

—JOAN BENOIT SAMUELSON

How to Train

8. *Run by Feel*

Take a moment and think about your friends who play ball sports. I wonder if you agree with the following: for them to reach a level of excellence in their sport, they have to hone certain skills. The basketball player has to be able to shoot and dribble, the softball player must hit and throw, the golfer must learn to accurately drive the ball and putt. To be excellent at a ball sport means you have to master several different skills.

What skills do you need to learn to reach your potential as a runner? I would argue there are mental skills like "keeping a calm mind," which my college coach would often say during challenging workouts. When someone suggests running is as simple as putting one foot in front of the other, they have a point. Yet you can make improvements in your posture, for example, especially when you get tired. (Though you'll need muscular strength to do that, so build that chassis!) But what else is there? Compared to the basketball player who has to learn to shoot, dribble, pass, rebound, and play defense, your list is probably shorter.

And at the top of the shorter list? I'd put "running by feel" every time.

Learning to run by feel is a critical skill if you want to become an excellent runner. It is crucial for race performance, especially in cross country. It is also crucial for your long-term development on the track. The connection may not be obvious at first, but learning to run by feel also improves your chances of staying injury-free.

The tricky thing is that running by feel is difficult for coaches to teach, and it will no doubt take you some time to learn—think months, not weeks. It also applies to many different aspects of your training.

The next time you put on your running shoes, imagine you're heading to a cross country meet. How hard should you run the first 200m, 400m, or 800m—especially when you won't likely hear any meaningful splits along the way? And even if you did get your splits, what would they mean if the course has thick grass? Or what if the course is muddy and you're running the fourth race of the day, after it's been torn up? Obviously, a 400m split on such a surface would mean something different than a 400m split early in a 3,200m track race.

When you're only 800m into a 5,000m cross country race, you have over two and a half miles to go: you need to balance your ideal position with the distance you have yet to cover—without decelerating each stride to the finish line. If you know how to run by feel, you're less likely go out too hard in the opening minutes. It's a skill worth learning!

If we zoom out and look at a week (or month) of training, running by feel will also help you do a couple of things. First, it'll help you to stay injury-free. Second, it can help you avoid overtraining. And both are keys to consistency.

Let's say you run a cross country race in spikes, in mid-September, four weeks from your championship season. Though you have followed a thoughtful progression of training, and though you have raced in these shoes before, you go home that night with sore calves. Or worse, your right Achilles is tender to the touch. What do you do? You might decide to do a bit of self-therapy (I offer some useful videos of self-therapy exercises on CoachJayJohnson. com/CIKbook), and you go to bed confident you'll be able to run the next day.

You join your team Saturday morning for practice, and you do your typical muscle activations and mobility exercises. You then do a 60-minute run, where you incorporate 5 x 20 seconds at 3,200m effort, starting at the 45-minute mark. You don't normally find this simple assignment difficult, but today you feel your right Achilles again in the first 10 minutes: it's not painful, but it's definitely tight. You continue to run, and at the 20-minute mark everything feels pretty good. You're talking with your friends and enjoying the morning, and before you know it, you're at 45 minutes. You do the first stride, and now your Achilles hurts a bit once more.

What should you do? Do you finish the run or do the next four strides with your teammates?

The novice runner might say to herself, "The assignment was five strides, so that's what I need to do." She'll likely do all five, even though her Achilles goes from slightly painful on the first one to quite painful by the fifth.

The runner who has dealt with niggles in the past may say, "Agggghhhh... I know I shouldn't run another one, but I'm going to anyway. If that one doesn't go well, I'll skip the last three." If this runner feels pain again on the second stride, he'll tend to make the smart decision and skip the rest.

In either case, the desire to become an excellent runner pushes the runner to do the strides—despite the pain. And while desire for excellence is an enviable trait, neither of these hypothetical athletes would be making the best decision.

When faced with this dilemma, the veteran runner would do some version of the following. After running the first stride, she'll simply say, "Shoot. I've got to shut this down and jog the rest of the way. My team needs me to be 100 percent four weeks from now. I'm frustrated, but I need to stay as consistent as possible. I'll ask my coach what I can do tonight to work on my Achilles."

Your goal is to become this type of runner—one who has the courage and patience to shut things down when you feel a niggle.

Some might say the veteran runner is simply the one who "pays attention to her body." And that's absolutely the case! The skill of running by feel in

Running by feel is a critical skill for race performance, especially in cross country.

workouts and races improves your ability to pay attention to the occasional niggle on easy days. However, "paying attention to your body" has its limitations, and doesn't necessarily lead to mastering the skill of running by feel.

A distance runner has to balance bodily discomfort while racing with being mindful about niggles during training. It's not an either/or situation. Your goal is not to have a mindset where you say, "I'm either grinding through training and racing or I'm casually running for fitness." You need a both/and approach: "I endure both discomfort in races and discomfort in shutting things down in practice when necessary. I'm willing to both run by feel during training and tell my coach about the occasional niggle."

Consistency and running by feel are tightly linked, because running by feel can keep you from overtraining. That means you'll "stay on top of your training and not buried under it." Those are the words of Sam Bell, who coached Bob Kennedy, the first person born outside of Africa to run under 13 minutes for 5,000m. When you can run by feel, you'll be able to train that next day and pay attention to your fatigue, possibly running a bit easier than you normally would (which can be a challenge as you'll want to go with your friends who are running their normal paces).

Finally, in high school sports, slogans like "no pain, no gain," "pain is just weakness leaving the body," and "go big or go home" are commonly used and can really shape how we think about training. You're going to be uncomfortable when racing, and obviously you'll be sweating. But let's remember that your goal is to train intelligently week after week so that you can run personal records throughout the season. Those slogans aren't applicable to the path you and your team are on, the path to greater levels of fitness that result in faster racing.

There are a number of specific workouts that can teach you to run by feel, and I'll share those in the following pages. The bottom line is that running by feel will allow you to string together sustained periods of injury-free, uninterrupted training, which invariably leads to fast racing and often to running PRs.

70

9. Do Easy Days Easy and Hard Days Hard

There is a very good chance that your coach assigns easy days and hard days throughout the week. You might also have medium days, but for the moment, let's assume there are just two types of days—easy and hard. (And we'll add races to the hard category.)

You need to alternate between hard and easy efforts.

When should you work out next?

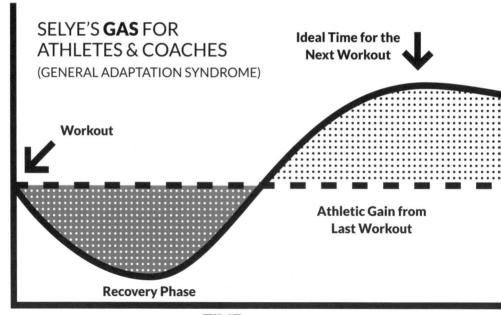

SELYE'S **GAS** FOR ATHLETES & COACHES
(GENERAL ADAPTATION SYNDROME)

Ideal Time for the Next Workout

Workout

Athletic Gain from Last Workout

Recovery Phase

TIME

As you know, you need time to recover from workouts or races, so you need to alternate between hard and easy efforts. When we graph the ideal flow of hard and easy days—over the course of a week, month, or even a season—we begin to understand how an athlete's body is recovering and adapting.

This graph draws on Dr. Hans Selye's research into what's known as the general adaptation syndrome. The dotted line is your baseline or starting fitness level. Some sort of stimulus is needed to kick-start adaptation and inch that fitness level up—in this case a workout or a race. But then there's a dip, which indicates your body isn't ready for the next stimulus. Instead, it needs time to recover.

SUPERCOMPENSATION

Post-Workout: Athlete is fully recovered and ready for the next training stimulus (workout).

Even if you're new to the sport, you intuitively know this to be true: if you race in the morning, your body probably doesn't want to race again that evening. The same goes for tough workouts: if you do a hard session Monday afternoon, your body probably doesn't want to do an even harder workout Tuesday morning. The consistent runner listens to his or her body!

The dip does not mean that you need a day of complete rest, of course. There's still work to be done. A recovery run is typically the best way to prepare for the following day's work, though in your first season of training these days may feel taxing. If your coach assigns a day off from running, you should follow his or her instructions. You may choose to do some mobility and flexibility exercises, however. Even a few minutes of that work will also help speed recovery—not hinder it.

The fun part of adaptation occurs during the so-called supercompensation phase. It's at this point that an athlete is ready for another hard workout, or even a race. Exactly how long does it take to reach the supercompensation phase? Or, in other words, when should you run your next workout or race? Any place along the bump in the graph is appropriate: if your body has returned to the dotted line, it has adapted to the stress of the previous effort. If we're trying to maximize training, though, the next workout would come near the top of the curve.

At the end of the day, you need to give your body enough time to recover. This varies from runner to runner. No athlete—aside from a handful of professionals—can do this with absolute precision. Almost every coach and every runner makes their best guess about recovery time, often based on months or years of personal experience.

Even the most experienced runner might fall into the trap of running too soon after his or her last hard day. You don't want to be that athlete. Instead, you want to be the runner who follows instructions on easy days, which will maximize your chances of recovering fully. And this will maximize your ability to run well in your next workout or race.

Everyone needs to balance hard efforts with easy ones, but it's especially true for high school athletes, and even more important for those who are new to the sport. Younger runners need to be patient, but they do have something in their back pocket: All runners will gain fitness on the harder days (and a race counts as the hardest day of any week). And while seasoned runners will mostly maintain fitness or recover on their easy days, younger athletes will continue to see small gains in fitness on theirs. Bonus for them! Easy days do not mean super-short practices or super-slow jogging—or days you can just skip. These are important "bridge days" between hard efforts, where you can check in with your body and get ready for the next workout or race. You still need to incorporate all the pre-run elements, including proper muscle activation and a dynamic warm up. You also should rev your engine with strides and strengthen the chassis with some general strength work.

Your coach will determine the effort and duration of your easy runs, which will allow you to recover. Your job is to enjoy the run (and be able to maintain a conversation with your teammates along the way), to focus while doing strides, and to take your pre- and post-run work seriously. Ideally, you will make minor improvements on easy days: maybe a bit more mobility and strength, maybe slightly faster strides, maybe better posture (which translates to biomechanical efficiency and faster races). Done right, recovery has a lot to give.

So do your easy days easy—and allow yourself to do your hard days hard. If ever in doubt, do less. If you and your coach notice that you're struggling in workouts, for example, or that you're more fatigued day to day than normal, it makes sense to back off and do less. Your coach may also notice that you're struggling in the occasional workout, and that you're running slower, not faster, as it progresses. Sometimes, you'll need to endure these sessions, but even older athletes, who are running higher mileage and doing intense workouts fairly regularly, might have a hard day cut short by a coach. Why? As my college coach often said, "You want to live to fight another day." If your coach ever does have you end a workout early, there is a chance you can still finish practice with some faster strides and some light general strength and mobility. Then go home and get some extra sleep (possibly for the next several nights).

Runners are competitive by nature, and you may want to compete with your teammates (or yourself) each and every day. But remember that the very best runners—whether they're in high school, in college, or have gone pro—know it's best to focus that competitive spirit. The best runners have found a way to balance their hard workouts and races with easy days that are, in fact, easy. Your overall fitness trend will be an upward one when you take a similar approach.

If ever in doubt, do less.

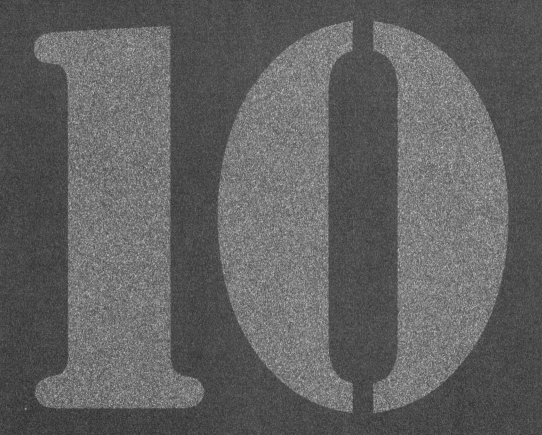

10. Practice Race Pace (or Faster)

Earlier, I said that one of the biggest mistakes I see high school athletes make is not running strides most days. Their other big mistake is not practicing race pace often enough. What's race pace? It's simply the pace you want to run for a given distance at a given time of year. In cross country, your ideal pace for 5,000m may vary slightly depending on the course—you'll most likely run a faster pace in a flat park and a slower one on a hilly golf course—but you'll have a general range in mind for the season. In track, your race pace will get faster as you move down from the 3,200m to 1,600m to 800m—even if your fitness level stays the same.

Most athletes do a great job building their aerobic engines in the off-season. We've discussed the importance of strengthening your chassis and revving your engine most days. Now it's time to get your legs ready to run fast for your entire race distance.

Many runners can work their hearts and lungs hard throughout a 5,000m cross country race, but their legs fail them in the final 1,600m, 800m, or even 400m. Practicing race pace helps eliminate that problem. If you have an important meet in mid-September, it's crucial that you've moved at your ideal race pace well before you get to the starting line. And it's wise to have run faster than race pace, so that when the gun goes off, the initial pace doesn't feel overwhelming.

You might separate race pace into two categories: date pace and goal pace. Bill Bowerman, the iconic University of Oregon coach and co-founder of Nike, popularized this important concept. Date pace is simply the pace that you can maintain in a race today. For instance, a girl who can run 5:20 for the 1,600m at the start of outdoor track, may be aiming for 5:14 by the end of the year. In this case, 5:20 would be her date pace and 5:14 her goal pace. She needs to run both in training, and she needs to run goal pace (or faster) in the very first week of outdoor track—if only for 100m or 200m at a time. Why? Because she can't expect to run 5:14 by the end of the season if she's only trained at 5:20 effort.

Let's break down the various paces this 5:14 hopeful needs to practice:

1,600m performance	400m pace	200m pace	100m pace
5:20	80 seconds	40 seconds	20 seconds
5:16	79 seconds	39.5 seconds	19.75 seconds
5:14	78.5 seconds	39.25 seconds	19.63 seconds
5:12	78 seconds	39 seconds	19.5 seconds

Notice the 5:12 pace, which, for every 400m, is 2 seconds faster than her goal pace. Practicing this speed will set her up to run at least 5:14. It will also mean that 5:14 pace won't feel overly fast in a race environment, especially that first lap. Whether she's running repeat 200s, 300s, 400s, or 500s, she needs to practice 19.5-second rhythm much of the year. Her date pace rhythm—20 seconds—simply won't get her to her goal pace.

Because that half second per 100m makes a big difference over 400m, it's crucial that both the athlete and the coach make running goal pace a priority. There are dozens of workouts to prepare a high school runner for the 1,600m—with repetitions ranging from 200m all the way up to a 1,000m time trial—and the training paces will vary workout to workout. The key, though, is to incorporate goal pace work right from the start—if only for 100m repeats at the beginning.

Practicing race pace is necessary for all events—from 800m to 3,200m on the track and in cross country. This means that a cross country runner who specializes in the 1,600m in the spring will run a variety of paces throughout the year: date pace and goal pace in cross country, plus date paces and goal paces for the 800m, 1,600m, and 3,200m. Remember, too, that date pace will change every few weeks as you gain fitness, so it's important to work with your coach as the season progresses.

11. Know That You Could Have Gone Farther or Faster (or Both)

Because we know that consistency in training is crucial for running PRs, we need to make sure that you're not racing in workouts. The consistent runner wants to run hard in workouts, while also holding back a bit. How do you make sure you're running hard enough to build your engine without running race effort in practice?

You need to finish workouts being able to say one of the following:

"I could have gone farther at the final pace if I had to. "

"I could have gone faster at the end if I needed to."

You should be able to say something along these lines at the end of almost every workout (the only exception being a time trial, where your coach instructs you to go "all out"). It's even better if you can say both—that you could have gone farther and gone faster. If you can finish a long run, for instance, knowing you could have gone another mile or two at a faster pace than you were running at the end, you have successfully completed a controlled run.

If you race workouts on a regular basis—if you're unable to go farther or faster—you won't be able to properly practice race effort. On occasion, you'll end a workout completely spent, especially if you're getting serious about training and are motivated to work hard. A dedicated athlete will almost certainly finish a calendar year with one or two workouts that accidentally became race efforts. But don't let that become your normal. If your Saturday long run turns into a long race, that's a more serious problem: your body isn't mature enough to handle the hard long runs that a collegiate or professional athlete might incorporate. If that happens, it's not the end of the world; you'll simply need more time to recover from the intense stimulus.

Keep on top of your training—not buried under it.

If you let yourself recover after accidentally running race effort in practice, you'll be ready for your next workout or race. And because high school athletes can often recover quickly compared to older athletes, you'll be back to 100 percent in no time (as long as racing a workout is the exception, not the rule). While most coaches can tell if an athlete has gone all out, and not run controlled, recovery is ultimately your responsibility. Don't be afraid of talking to your coach at the end of practice: "I ran all out today, coach. I know that wasn't the point of the workout, and I wanted to let you know. I look forward to executing the workout correctly the next time. Is there anything extra I need to do to recover from today?" You want to run PRs and your coach wants you to run PRs, so this type of communication is crucial for you to be ready to train or race at full strength as soon as possible.

How does the principle of farther or faster relate to consistency? Simple. It means that you ran controlled. Running controlled for weeks at a time, with meets being the only days you run all out, gives you a better chance of staying injury-free and, ultimately, running fast races. It helps ensure that you're "on top of your training and not buried under it." Remember, you have a finite amount of energy for training. Your academic workload and family obligations put limits on how much sleep you can get during the week. Combine those two factors, and it's crucial that while you train hard, you keep your workouts and long runs controlled so you are ready for what's next.

12. Prepare for Running Fast, Faster, Fastest

One of the keys to realizing your potential is the ability to speed up at the end of a race. While there may be a time or two in your junior or senior year where you run a great race by grinding out a hard pace right from the start, most often you'll perform your best when you complete the last half of the race faster than the first. This is what's known as running a negative split. You want to have the ability to "switch gears," whether that be moving up through the pack in cross country or passing a runner with 200m to go on the track.

You don't need to speed up in the middle of a race to run negative splits: you just need to run the last 400m, 200m, or even 100m faster than you were previously going. Most world records for distances a mile and up—and most high school personal records 1,600 and up—have been set through negative splits. In almost every race you run, you'll have competitors capable of running negative splits, and you need to be ready to do the same.

One way to ensure that you run negative splits is to speed up three times during a race. In the majority of races, your goal should be to run a given pace, then go fast, then go faster, and then go your fastest. This is a simple strategy,

Fast,
faster
fa

yet it's a hard one to execute. You'll need to practice it in workouts to properly execute it when it counts. There are two basic ways you can approach "fast, faster, fastest" in workouts.

Let's say you have a workout of 10 x 400m with 45 to 60 seconds recovery. Ideally, you'll run similar splits for the first seven repetitions, but on the eighth, ninth, and tenth, you successively increase your speed—going fast, faster, fastest. You don't want to run slow on the first seven 400s, but you'll need to find that edge between discomfort and control, so that you can confidently accelerate over the last three sets. If your workout is something like 6 x 1,000m, you can apply the same principle: maintain a relatively even pace over the first three repetitions, and then go fast, faster, fastest to finish the workout.

You can even apply this same principle to your last repeat. Ideally, as you cover the last 100m to 200m of your final repetition, you will practice switching gears. Yes, you'll be tired, but this is exactly what you have to do in a race. You want the experience of switching gears when tired, so it is more manageable, almost instinctive, on race day.

Let's assume you're preparing for a 1,600m race. Your coach might want you to go fast, faster, fastest in the final 500m. In the first 100m to 200m of this hypothetical race, he or she might encourage you to establish a position within the pack. This may be on the shoulder of the leader or near the back of the lead group. You'll likely get a 200m split from one of your coaches or teammates, or perhaps you'll hear feedback on your position. From there, you may be aiming for certain splits at 400m and 800m, or you may be going for a certain position. Either way, your coach wants you to approach the final 500m with fast, faster, fastest in mind, specifically fast for 200m, faster for 200m, and fastest for the last 100m of the race.

Envision this: You're coming into the homestretch before the bell lap. Rather than wait for the final 400m, you start to move up. This is the start of your 200m fast section. When you hit the backstretch, with 300m to the finish, you speed up again—initiating your faster segment. At this point, you're running hard, and you're uncomfortable. But because you've practiced switching gears, you're confident you can endure the discomfort a bit longer. You and your legs both know you can do this! When you come off the final turn and into the home-stretch, you have one last gear. You run your fastest 100m right at the end. Executing such a race plan—where you run a challenging pace for 1,100m and then go fast, faster, fastest in the last 500m—will more often than not lead to a great race. It's also how you can set yourself up for PR performances.

The 1,600m scenario we just walked through does not necessarily mean you'll win, but there are many ways to measure a great performance. If you

Practice switching gears when tired, so you will be ready to do it on race day.

consistently incorporate fast, faster, fastest, you'll consistently beat quite a few competitors and consistently turn in races you can be proud of.

Of course, you may be running against someone who has also read the last several paragraphs, and who is trying to execute a very similar strategy. Put another way, you should expect your competition to speed up alongside you. If that's the case, and even if you don't find yourself passing competitors on the backstretch, keep focused on shifting gears. Sometimes you may not beat someone ahead of you, but you end up beating your previous personal record. Don't get frustrated!

In a 3,200m race, you might follow a similar plan over the last 500m. Or the plan might focus on fast, faster, fastest with 800m to go: speeding up for 400m, then again for 200m, and finally once more over the last 200m. Taking a simple 100m/100m/100m approach with the last 300m of a 1,600m or 3,200m is another useful strategy—especially if you're new to track and don't have much experience changing gears when you're fatigued. In cross country, you might shift gears in the final 1,000m of a race, running fast, faster, fastest for 600m, 200m, and another 200m, respectively. No matter the distance, the key is that you and your coach have a general plan, with the caveat that you may need to move up in the pack before you execute your fast, faster, fastest segments—so that you're in contact with your target group.

There is an exception to running negatives splits: Most of the time for high school runners, negative splits are not ideal in the 800m. You and your competition will run the vast majority of your PRs with even or positive splits (where the first half of the race is slightly faster than the second). For 800m specialists, the first 200m is often the fastest. If you're reading this and your best event is the 800m, you'll still benefit from the fast, faster, fastest pattern in workouts. But when you're racing two laps, don't expect your last 200m to be your fastest.

There's one simple thing worth remembering: you can't execute a fast, faster, fastest finish to a race if you haven't practiced switching gears throughout the year. Your coach should design workouts that put you in a position to rehearse this skill over and over, so that when the gun goes off you're ready.

"*Determine to pay the price of a worthy goal. The trials you encounter will introduce you to your strengths.*"

Workouts

In a book about running, it's important to discuss some of the workout types you and your coach may choose throughout the year. But in a way, this is the least important section of the book. If you follow the first 12 points we've discussed, and embrace the three that come after this section, you'll have a great chance of staying injury-free and racing fast. It's also important to remember that while this book can teach you a lot about running, I'm not your coach. You should believe in your coach and follow his or her program to the letter. Why? Because you've got to trust the training you're doing if you want to race to your potential.

Here's how we're going to approach workouts: no matter the workout, there are a few variables worth considering, including frequency, distance or time, and intensity, along with the underlying rationale—or *the why am I doing this?* Even as workouts change throughout the year, these key variables don't.

Workouts vary between seasons for the simple reason that racing 5,000m on a grassy and possibly hilly course is different than running the 1,600m on a flat, responsive track. Within any given season, certain sessions are great for the first three weeks but not ideal for the last three. And no matter the workout, a simple test should always apply: Could I have run farther or faster (or both)? If the answer is yes, you're on your way to beneficial consistency. If the answer is no, you should practice more control.

Most good programs—those that are competitive at the state and national level—incorporate most of the following workouts in one form or another. But again, things will always vary from school to school, town to town.

LONG RUNS

Rationale: The long run is one of the best ways to develop your aerobic engine. It can be the cornerstone of a training program, or it can be something your coach assigns during the off-season and then removes once the season starts.

Frequency: Most programs have a long run scheduled every seven to 10 days throughout the year (though they may skip over it the week of a key race).

Distance or Time: For decades, high school runners were advised to incorporate long runs that represented 20 percent of their total weekly volume. The runner who ran 40 miles a week would do an eight-mile run, while the 50-mile-a-week runner was assigned 10. Today, however, most successful programs target a long run that's a bit over 20 percent of the weekly total, with many athletes logging a nine- or 10-mile run as part of their 40-mile weeks (so up to 25 percent).

You've got to trust the training you're doing if you want to race to your potential.

Some programs will assign target minutes instead of target miles. If an athlete happens to have a tough day, the thinking goes in a minute-based program, he or she can still feel good about logging a challenging run as long as he or she completes the assigned time. On a day that is windy, or one where you're dealing with rain or snow, running by minutes also makes a lot of sense, which is one reason many coaches will use both minutes and miles at different times of the year.

Intensity: Some programs simply aim to log a certain volume and don't focus on intensity. Others prefer a challenging pace, especially in the last third of the long run. Some programs do a progression long run, where the pace quickens throughout the workout. A 75-minute assignment might include 25 minutes easy, 25 minutes a bit faster (yet still comfortable), and a final 25 minutes at a challenging pace. Regardless, the concept of "long, slow distance" that was popular decades ago—where the focus was on building distance throughout the year, with running so slow that "jogging" best described it—is dead. Today, the best programs in the country *do not* have their runners shuffling through long runs at a slow pace. While some programs may have a relaxed long or long-ish run 24 or 48 hours following an important race, the pace is easy—but not slow.

The Test: If your answer to the "farther or faster (or both)" test is no, your coach will likely shorten your next long assignment and encourage you to go easier for the first two-thirds of the run. Trust this adjustment and know that when you've completed a few weeks of solid long runs, you'll be ready for a modest increase in time or distance.

FARTLEK RUNS

Rationale: Fartlek runs are continuous efforts that athletes have used to build their engines for decades. The Swedish word "fartlek" means "speed play," and it describes a workout in which you oscillate between multiple paces—at least two. Typically, when a coach has 20 or 40 or even more athletes running a workout at the same time, he or she will assign two durations and two suggestions for effort—the "on" portion and the "steady" portion. Fartleks sound simple, but if done properly, they are not easy workouts.

Frequency: Most coaches that use fartlek runs assign them every two to three weeks in the summer, and once again in the winter. Other coaches make these workouts a weekly staple throughout the year.

Distance or Time: At the start of the cross country season, a typical workout might be 6 x 2 minutes "on," 3 minutes "steady," for a total of 30 minutes: where the on and steady portion add up to 5 minutes. You simply run 2 minutes on, followed by 3 minutes at a steady pace. Young athletes may do as little as

The best programs in the country do not have their runners shuffling through long runs.

20 minutes of fartlek, while older athletes may do 45 minutes or more.

Intensity: What exactly is "steady"? It's faster than your easy pace but typically slower than your 5,000m pace (though later in the year, it could be 5,000m effort or faster). And that's the magic of the fartlek—a continuous run where you familiarize yourself with solid efforts during the steady segments. What makes this workout challenging is not the "on" portions, but the steady portions. For example, if you're a 20-minute 5,000m runner, the 2-minute "on" portion is only a tenth of your race distance. For a 16-minute 5,000m runner, 2 minutes on is still only an eighth of a cross country course.

The Test: Ask yourself, "What is a steady pace that I can run for 3 minutes in a controlled fashion, with good posture? And how many 5-minute sets can I run and still pass the 'farther or faster (or both)' test?"

Here's a simple fartlek workout: Six or eight sets of 2 minutes on, 3 minutes steady, for a total of 30 or 40 minutes. Not only will you benefit from a sustained aerobic effort, but you'll also rehearse 5,000m effort, which prepares your legs for racing. This workout is about feel, so target perceived effort, not a specific pace. Instead of constantly checking your GPS watch, hone your ability to run by feel.

Let's say you get three sets into a 30-minute fartlek run and you can't maintain your "on" or "steady" paces during the remaining sets. With this type of workout, that's absolutely fine, especially as you master fartlek running. It takes time to learn where that edge is between running controlled and running a race effort—when you can feel that the metallic taste in your mouth or the burning sensation in your lungs.

PROGRESSION RUNS

Rationale: Progression runs are another great way to build your aerobic engine, though they must be executed correctly. It's easy to run too fast in a progression run; instead, aim for something that's quite controlled.

Frequency: These can be done every other week during the season, but as with fartlek workouts, some coaches make this a weekly workout only during the summer and winter.

Distance or Time: Progression runs can be as short as 20 minutes or as long as an hour, yet typically they will be between 30 and 40 minutes.

Intensity: Start at a solid pace, then slowly speed up as you go, ending with a challenging pace. The key is that the challenging miles are nowhere near race effort.

The Test: If you properly execute a progression run, you'll be glad the run is over. As always, "farther or faster (or both)" must apply.

The first few times you do a progression run, it may make sense to have an assignment such as 10 minutes steady, 10 minutes faster, 5 minutes fast but controlled. Older athletes can start with 10/10/5/5, with the understanding that the first two 10-minute segments will be very controlled. And depending on the program and time of year, coaches might assign progression runs that are much longer than 30 minutes. In some programs, the weekly long run becomes a progression run.

After you've done a few progression runs, you and your teammates might want to run by feel and let things unfold naturally, gently squeezing down the pace while keeping everything controlled. If you end up bent over, hands on your knees, you probably ran too hard. That's not the end of the world, but you have to remember that it can take several days to recover from a progression run that accidentally turns into a race. If you embrace the idea that consistency is key, you simply want to get in a solid effort, recover for a day, and then be ready for the next important run or workout 48 hours later.

THRESHOLD RUNS

Rationale: Most scientists and coaches agree that a threshold run—which some people refer to as a tempo run or a steady-state run—is the fastest you can run without producing a significant amount of lactate. Professional athletes might take advantage of laboratory tests to know exactly how fast that is. But for the vast majority of runners, including high school runners, that pace emerges from running by feel.

Frequency: This is another workout that is often done every two or three weeks, but, again, some coaches use this as a weekly cornerstone in the summer and winter. Many programs use threshold runs throughout the year, including the competitive season.

Distance or Time: While professional runners can run this pace for up to an hour, most high school runners will run between 20 minutes and 30 minutes for their threshold runs (though some may run as long as 45 minutes). Many coaches like "broken" thresholds, an example being a 20-minute threshold broken into two 10-minute segments, with 2 to 3 minutes of easy jogging for a short recovery.

Intensity: This is a challenging run, but it must be controlled. Otherwise, it's not a threshold run. If your hands are on your knees at the end and you don't want to do the necessary engine-revving work to finish the day, then you've run too hard. The best way for athletes to run this as a group is to ensure that everyone is running below their threshold pace, which may mean that the run is easier for the fittest team members. That's fine: those athletes still get a great aerobic stimulus, and will feel recovered and ready to handle the next workout or race.

It takes time to learn where that edge is between running controlled and running a race effort.

The Test: This is a simple one. You want to get near, but not over, the edge where you experience the telltale signs of lactate.

How long can you hold threshold pace? It depends on your training age and your fitness. A freshman who is just getting into shape might be able to manage two miles at threshold pace, while a senior returning for his or her fourth year might be able to run many more. Ultimately, there is a wide range of distances and durations that are appropriate for everyone on your team. A threshold run can just as easily be assigned by minutes rather than miles—either way makes sense.

VARIATIONS

In addition to long runs, fartlek runs, progression runs, and threshold runs, which are all fairly popular, there are other aerobic workouts that you and your coach might consider.

Progression Fartlek: The concept is simple—the pace of the "on" segments gets faster with each set. During a normal fartlek run, an athlete ideally runs a consistent "on" pace, but might gradually increase the speed of the steady portions as the run progresses. For most high school athletes, it's more exciting to make successive "on" portions faster—but still controlled—bit by bit.

Aerobic Repeats: There are two elements to the aerobic repeat. The first is that these are long—at least 2 or 3 minutes (covering at least 600m). Many coaches like assigning 800m, 1,000m, and 1,600m repeats. You might go as high as 2,000m. The second element is that the majority of the repeat is run aerobically, which means controlled. Then it's fine to feel the telltale signs of lactate production over the last 10 percent or so of the repetition. You'll have some amount of recovery between the repetitions, and you'll be ready for the next one. These are typically challenging workouts and typically come after a few weeks of the aerobic workouts we've discussed.

With any of these workouts, you'll know you've done them correctly when you can do another workout 48 hours later and feel good. There may be times when you feel sluggish even after 48 hours, but that should be the exception, not the rule. Again, you want to be on top of your training, not buried under it.

"Expect the river to be wild, surprising and challenging. To expect the opposite is to live in delusion."

—SENECA

Racing

Racing is a special opportunity and one you should look forward to. The chance to toe the line with your friends in the fall, and the opportunity to race against your competitors and against the clock in track, is unique. While you may choose to run after high school, it's common for an athlete who races in college to have a true soft spot for their prep days. Even most adult runners miss their high school careers. As a teenager, you have a truly unique opportunity to compete.

You need to do two things race to your potential. First, you have to learn how to be uncomfortable. Specifically, you must learn how to maintain race pace while dealing with the discomfort. Second, you want to speed up at the end of the race. This simple task is the fundamental challenge to competition, and it's difficult to execute. If you wake up on race day with the simple *intention* of running hard in final the stretch, you'll likely improve your ability to do so. And you can practice this intention in workouts. Say to yourself, "I'm going to be uncomfortable, but this is an opportunity to improve my ability to deal with discomfort. I can do this, and if I do this, I'll eventually race faster." Finally, you can build these two abilities month after month, season after season—just like you can build your aerobic engine.

A handful of basic tools and mental reminders can teach you ways of dealing with discomfort.

Two of the most successful coaches in the history of American distance running are Mark Wetmore and Jerry Schumacher. Coach Wetmore often tells his athletes to "keep a calm mind" during their most intense workouts. Why? Because once an athlete internalizes those four words, he or she has a much better chance of running a great race. While it's difficult to keep a calm mind at the start of a large cross country race, it's crucial that you do so. Young runners, in particular, will often get caught up in the pre-race hype and excitement and run their first 3 minutes much too fast. They suffer mid-race and can dramatically slow down in the final minutes before crossing the finish line. Instead, be smart, keep a calm mind, and execute the type of race plan we talk about elsewhere in this book, a plan that likely has you running hard but controlled for at least the first half (though this may not be true for a skilled upperclassman who may be instructed to run aggressively from the start).

Coach Schumacher tells his athletes, "You have to get comfortable being uncomfortable." That's fantastic advice. If you want to run to your fitness level, pass as many competitors as you can, and race to a PR, you'll have to run fast while you're uncomfortable—there is no other way. As the saying goes, "Simple ain't easy." But if you can do this simple thing—being comfortable with the discomfort—you'll race to your potential. No one starts their racing career as an expert at staying calm and embracing the discomfort. You have to learn both. Your goal is to make progress—with each hard workout and with each race—toward becoming an athlete who can be extremely uncomfortable during a race and have the mental composure to focus in the final minutes in cross country or in the final few hundred meters on the track.

In fact, having the right mental composure will start days before the meet. If we work backwards from the race—three, five or even seven days out—you should do some visualization. This simply means that you'll see yourself running the race in your mind. Some teams do this as part of a weekly practice, while other athletes do it at home. Get comfortable—you can lay on the floor, your bed, or sit in a chair. Ideally, your surroundings will be quiet, but that's not mandatory (though at least put your phone away). I had the best success as a collegiate athlete when I'd commit several minutes to watch the race unfold in my mind, from start to finish. As we got closer to race day, I'd lengthen my visualizations to 10 minutes.

The first few days, I'd see the ideal race unfold and feel myself dealing with discomfort. I was always able to endure the pace and speed up at the end. After I felt confident I could do that in the race, I'd add one or two wrinkles to my visualization. For instance, I might see competitors surge in the middle of the race, leaving me to decide if I could go with them and maintain that increased pace. I'd always end those versions in the same way—with me enduring the mid-race discomfort and speeding up at the end. Science backs up the importance of visualization, and you can read articles about it on my website. But my firsthand experience is simple enough: my best racing was always preceded by a few days of visualization.

Even with the best preparations—mental and physical—most athletes struggle to master the skill of racing fast when they're uncomfortable. I'll be blunt: your best race is going to hurt. There is no time like the present to learn, in each race, where your edge of discomfort is and get right up to it. Your best racing will not come easy. You'll have to endure a great deal of discomfort if you want to race to your potential. But there is something remarkable about testing yourself on race day, and seeing where your own limitations are. You can truly surprise yourself! And you can do that by building your abilities season over season, even month over month.

Value incremental progress. We know fitness gains aren't linear, and growing your capacity to endure discomfort will not be linear either. However, over the course of your career, you can become an athlete who is fiercely competitive, a teammate who can be counted on, and a runner who often runs your best race on the most important day of the season.

No one starts out as an expert at staying calm and embracing discomfort. You have to learn both.

"Simple ain't easy."

—THELONIUS MONK

Support Your Training

13. Remember to Sleep

What's the least exciting ingredient in the recipe to becoming an excellent high school runner? Sleep. You want to train hard so that you can race fast—that's the fun stuff! To absorb your training gains and recover from racing, however, you have to sleep. This is how you will gain fitness over the course of the season.

Sleep is like a secret ingredient in the recipe of running success.

As a high school runner, you need enough sleep to support the training your coach assigns you, to support the physical growth of adolescence, and to support academic performance. Because you're making demands on your body every day in practice, you're going to need more sleep than your non-running classmates. Your job is to find another 20 or 30 or 45 minutes in your already hectic schedule for sleep.

Paul Vandersteen coaches the boy's team at Neuqua Valley High School, in Naperville, Illinois. He is a great coach with a number of useful resources for his athletes, including an approach to "championship sleep."

Neuqua Valley Men's Cross Country & Track and Field						
WHAT TIME SHOULD YOU GO TO BED?						
Wake-up Time						
5:30am	6:00am	6:30am	7:00am	7:30am	8:00am	8:30am
Bed Time						
Awful 10:30pm	11:00pm	11:30pm	12:00am	12:30am	1:00am	1:30am
Bad 10:00pm	10:30pm	11:00pm	11:30pm	12:00am	12:30am	1:00am
Minimal 9:30pm	10:00pm	10:30pm	11:00pm	11:30pm	12:00am	12:30am
Mediocre 9:00pm	9:30pm	10:00pm	10:30pm	11:00pm	11:30pm	12:00am
Good 8:30pm	9:00pm	9:30pm	10:00pm	10:30pm	11:00pm	11:30pm
Champion 8:15pm	8:30pm	9:00pm	9:30pm	10:00pm	10:30pm	11:00pm

This table is brutally honest with the numbers. You know when you need to wake up, so you can work backwards and see what time you need to go to bed. And the lesson is a clear one: you can't expect to be a good or champion runner if you're getting an awful or minimal amount of sleep week after week. If you have a day or two where you get mediocre or even bad sleep, just don't let it become a habit. With sleep, you can get back on track and string together several good nights of consistency-building rest.

You're in high school. Of course, you will have a night here or there where you either go to bed late or sleep poorly. You might have to study late for an important test. You might get home late from a track meet. There are days when you have to get up much earlier than normal. The key with sleep is that you're as consistent as possible, and that you get enough rest to support your training, your physical growth, and your academic workload.

Sleep may not be all that exciting, but it is like a secret ingredient in the recipe of running success. It does wonders. And no, you can't make up for a week's worth of bad sleep by sleeping in really late on Saturday or Sunday morning.

Think of running and then think of lifting weights. Which one builds you up? Lifting weights, of course. The term "anabolic" literally means "building up." The chassis-building work we've covered is anabolic. After an hour of sleep, your body releases signaling molecules that also build you up—

testosterone and human growth hormone, or HGH, that all athletes, regardless of age or gender, need to strengthen their chassis. The more sleep, the more your body releases these important substances that basically say, time to repair yourself!

The opposite of anabolic is catabolic, which means "breaking down." Running is a catabolic activity. On the micro-level, it literally tears your muscles down. If you get ample sleep, however, your body can rebuild itself. Most athletes—from middle school runners all the way to professional runners—find that they need more sleep as they train harder. This is because they have more and more rebuilding that needs to be done each day.

You might be thinking, "Got it. I need to sleep. If I'm honest, I need more sleep. But sometimes, I have a hard time sleeping. What do I do then?" If that's the case, you want to maximize the quality of the sleep you do get.

That's where the concept of sleep hygiene comes in. The first time I heard this term, I thought "like dental hygiene," and that's not too far off the mark. In the same way you have a routine for taking care of your teeth, you need a routine to allow your body to fall asleep. High school student-athletes need sleep hygiene to support their training, their physical growth during adolescence, and the significant challenges of high school academics.

Admittedly, sleep hygiene is a little bit like flossing. You may not like it at first, but it can have a dramatic impact. So it's best to establish the routine and stick to it.

What's not to like about sleep hygiene? Well, you need to stay off your phone at night. That's because your phone emits light—so-called blue light—that is different than the light in your bedroom. Your tablet, your computer, and your TV also emit it. Blue light throws off your body's internal clock, or circadian rhythm. And this is very disruptive to your ability to fall asleep and to the quality of the sleep you do get. Compromise either of those, and you won't be rebuilding your muscles fully.

As with many things related to running, the solution to a disrupted circadian rhythm is simple but not easy. Choose to make the 60 to 90 minutes before bed screen-free. I know you're thinking, "How the heck am I going to be able to do that?" At first, it'll be a hard habit to establish. But like flossing, it'll be good for you—and good for your running. Putting your phone away an hour or so before bed is a small choice, but one that will have a big impact on your training and racing—regardless of your genetic ability.

Sleep more. Sleep better.

And each night will lead to solid training and faster racing.

14. Don't Forget Nutrition

Now that you're on board with making sleep a priority, it's time to remember that to train well and race fast you'll have to fuel your body with nutritious foods. While you don't need a complete overhaul of your diet to train at a high level and stay injury-free, you do need to eat better than your typical class-mate. It's a pretty simple equation: as an athlete you'll need more whole foods and fewer processed ones. You can't train optimally if all you eat is fast food. The same goes for highly processed protein bars. Take a cue from the best athletes in the world, who often show their meals on social media—big plates of fruits, vegetables, and other unprocessed foods. That's not to say you can't have fun along the way. Many of these same world-class athletes balance their healthy eating with the occasional treat: donuts for marathoner Molly Huddle and ice cream for track star Shelby Houlihan.

Let's go back to the car analogy and ask a simple question: How do you want to fuel your engine? Most of the time you want the word "nutritious" to describe your fuel, just as a high-performance sportscar needs high-octane gasoline. But "most of the time" does not mean "all of the time," and it's crucial that you don't impose overly rigid rules around eating. Don't let others impose them on you either.

The standard American diet often does not include the necessary nutrition for great athletes. Just like there's a balance between hard days and easy days, there is a balance between eating like your peers who aren't athletes and eating like the world's best athletes. What should this balance look like? For every instance that you eat processed food—perhaps from a fast food restaurant or a convenience store—you want to balance that with a meal that is nutritious, which probably means a meal prepared at home. Every family has different routines around meals, and coaches may or may not have detailed suggestions for how you can support your training. Regardless, if the word "nutritious" applies to your meals and snacks more often than not, you're probably striking the right balance. If you're thinking lots of vegetables, you're right. You might also add to the list good sources of fats likes nuts and avocados. And you'll need plenty of protein, which might take the form of animal proteins or plant-based—like hummus, tofu, or beans. Carbohydrate intake is vital if you're going to train optimally, with some research showing endurance athletes need a lot more carbs than the rest of the population. (For detailed suggestions, visit CoachJayJohnson.com/CIKbook.)

Where do most high school athletes make mistakes with food? That's simple: they don't eat enough to support the two things that are happening with their bodies. Your growing physically, which requires proper nutrition. And you're training hard, which requires a lot of food—more than a non-athlete needs.

124

What happens if you don't eat enough? You'll be fatigued at school, for one thing, and you'll be exhausted after practices and races. While your young body is resilient, there is no need to tolerate this type of life—so eat!

If you continually fail to properly fuel your body, you might experience relative energy deficiency in sport—or RED-S. It doesn't matter if you're a boy or a girl; if you don't eat the right amount of food, you won't perform at your best levels.

Finally, there are well-intentioned adults that forget that what is best for them when it comes to nutrition may not be best for you. The author Michael Pollan has a simple suggestion for adults: "Eat food. Mostly Plants. Not too much." Working backwards, obviously the last sentence does not apply to you—you need to eat a lot of food. "Mostly plants" is something that you and your parents can discuss. When he says "eat food," he's talking about choosing whole foods over the processed ones we're presented with daily. And that's good advice. At the end of the day, try your best to find a balance between the normal high school diet and a diet that's similar to elite athletes.

15. *Listen to Your Body*

In this book's preface, I said that it's not my opinion, but rather a fundamental principle, that a block of injury-free training, with thoughtful workouts and adequate recovery, will almost always lead to good performances. We have discussed two elements in training—strengthening the chassis and running by feel—that, when done well, will increase your chances of staying injury-free. We've also established that you must learn to deal with discomfort when you're racing or doing hard workouts. The next skill you need to learn is how to distinguish between the soreness that is part of training and the pain that could indicate the beginning of an injury. This sounds like a simple distinction, but it's often a hard one to make.

Essentially, what you're trying to identify is a "niggle," that odd-sounding word again that many runners use to describe something that's not a full-blown injury but something that is uncomfortable and may keep them from training at 100 percent. It's almost unheard of for a high school athlete to run for four years without a few niggles, yet there is no reason you can't train and race for weeks or months at a time without one popping up.

If you take one thing from this section, it's this: learn to identify a niggle, tell your coach whenever you have one, and be willing to follow his or her advice for getting through it (which may include doing additional soft-tissue or mobility work outside of practice). Your coach may or may not adjust training; don't be concerned if he or she tells you not to run for a day or two. Of course, one would rather be 100 percent all of the time, but when the time comes that you have a niggle, you have to have the maturity to ask, "What do I need to do to keep this from becoming an injury?"

The first opportunity to identify a niggle is in your pre-run routine. What's sore? Is anything painful? As you go through either your team's pre-run routine, or the exercises in the videos that accompany this book, you'll want to pay attention to how you feel. During most weeks of training, you can expect to have a bit of soreness, and a bit of fatigue, especially after hard workouts—that's fine. You won't need to do anything different than your coach's assignment for the day. You're on the lookout for significant discomfort or pain.

When practice is over and you head home, take a couple of moments to take a mini-inventory of your body. How do your calves and Achilles tendons feel? What about your quads and hamstrings? And is there anything you can do at home to ensure you'll stay injury-free? If you do this inventory daily, you greatly decrease the chance of injury, in addition to learning what your typical problem areas are.

Make sure that you don't overwhelm yourself with a lengthy to-do list of soft-tissue work and mobility exercises. You don't want to have those essential activities turn into things you dread. One of the best coaches in the country, John O'Malley, the boy's coach at Sandburg High School, in Illinois, gave a group of his veteran athletes the option of "homework" at the start of a cross country season. It consisted of mobility exercises that could be done in just 5 minutes, and ended up being a great success. His rationale was simple: do this work in the evening to be better prepared for the next day's run.

Sandburg athletes took their homework to another level. They began to post photos to the team's text thread to confirm they had done their assignments—and to motivate teammates to do theirs. Together, they invested in their team's success. They didn't want to let each other down by skipping the small stuff and possibly missing a training session or two because of a niggle.

Even if you don't set up a group text, there are numerous exercises and soft-tissue techniques that you can do to stay injury-free (again, check out my website for explanatory videos). The key is that you acknowledge that you'll likely have a niggle at some point during a season; know that you can address it by following your coach's directions and by doing work outside of practice to get back to 100 percent. Niggles are going to happen, but much of the time you and your coach can prevent them from becoming injuries.

Throughout this book, I've discussed many ways of becoming an excellent high school runner. I'd like to close by sharing how some of the best programs—programs that consistently win state meets and Nike Cross Nationals—train. All of these programs utilize some of the key concepts in this book, but each has a training element or a team culture element that is unique. You should know that you, your coach, and your teammates can come up with a winning recipe that fits your unique environment, just as these programs have.

Putting It All into Practice

Naperville North Girls Team

School: **Naperville North High School**

Town: **Naperville, Illinois**

Enrollment: **2,825**

Team Composition: **Girls**

Coach: **Dan Iverson**

Team Size: **70 (cross country); 55 (outdoor track)**

Classification: **3A (largest classification)**

What have they accomplished? Nine state championships in cross country. Nine NXN appearances, finishing in the top four at NXN four times (2005, 2014, 2017, and 2018). Three Footlocker Finalists.

How do they build the engine? Not only do the girls complete long runs, they do progression long runs. They also do four-mile tempo runs. Coach Iverson uses a nine-day "micro-cycle" rather than the seven-day cycle, which means that over the course of the season, there isn't a set day for the long run or race-pace work.

How do they strengthen the chassis? The girls do some sort of yoga daily. At least twice a week, they do hurdle-mobility and mini-band work, as well as

Not only do the girls complete long runs, they do progression long runs.

rope stretching (active isolated flexibility). The sessions in the weight room take roughly 30 minutes, with the deadlift being a key part of their strength training.

How do they rev the engine? Almost everyday, the girls run strides or run through wickets (mini-hurdles). Once during each nine-day micro-cycle, they do "max speed," which in their case is "flying 30s." They also do plyometric work one day per micro-cycle.

Coach Iverson insists that each girl keeps a weekly training log. It's so important to him that if athletes don't turn in their logs, they can't practice. All Naperville North students have access to a classroom management system, and it's via this system that the athletes log their training.

The team has a long list of non-running, team-building opportunities throughout the year. The entire cross country team does a camping trip in August. A smaller group of about 30 athletes does a 270-mile relay in northern Michigan each summer. During the year, they will often play a running-based game on recovery days. Each fall, they have a 3,200m time trial, which they call the Monster Dash, because the girls warm up and cool down in their Halloween costumes.

"We try to be serious about running hard," Coach Iverson says. "Running a lot, and having fun."

"We try to be serious about running hard, running a lot, and having fun."

Loudoun Valley Boys and Girls Team

> **School:** **Loudoun Valley High School**
>
> **Town:** **Purcellville, Virginia**
>
> **Enrollment:** **1,390 students**
>
> **Team Composition:** **Combined**
>
> **Coaches:** **Joan and Marc Hunter**
>
> **Team Size:** **55 girls and 70 boys (cross country);**
> **55 girls and 70 boys (outdoor track)**
>
> **Classification:** **4A (third largest classification,**
> **with 6A being the largest)**

What have the boys accomplished? NXN champions in 2017 and 2018. Set the NXN record for lowest point total with 77 points in 2018. Five consecutive state cross country titles, scoring 15, 16, and 17 points in at the last three state meets. National records for the indoor 4 x 1,600m and indoor distance medley relay.

What have the girls accomplished? Two state cross country titles, three individual state champions. In 2019, they won the NXR South meet and finished tenth at NXN.

Twice a week, Loudon Valley uses wickets (or mini-hurdles), to improve running mechanics and speed.

How do they build the engine? The teams do weekly long runs in the summer and throughout the cross country season. Typically, these are run at a moderate pace, but sometimes they'll do a progression long run.

The bread-and-butter workout for Loudon Valley involves "critical velocity" repetitions, with CV pace being what an athlete could run for a 30- to 35-minute road race. They determine an athlete's CV pace with an online calculator, which uses an athlete's 3,200m or 5,000m time as its key input. Athletes new to the program may start with only 400m at CV pace; most athletes, however, do repetitions of 800m to 1,000m. The top athletes will do 6–7 x 800m or 1,000m, typically with a 200m recovery jog (less than 90 seconds). Other engine-building workouts include repeat miles at threshold pace (three or four repetitions) and threshold runs of 15 to 30 minutes.

How do they strengthen the chassis? To prevent injuries and improve strength, the Hunters are committed to doing work both before and after each day's run. They incorporate "prehab" in their dynamic warm-up routine, as well as joint rotations, postural work, lunge matrices, and balance work. They often end their training with bodyweight work, or with resistance-band work for those athletes who aren't ready for the weight room. More mature athletes lift two or three times a week, going through several single-leg exercises and doing more advanced lifts like hex bar deadlifts. Weight room work never takes more than 30 minutes. A series of hurdle-mobility exercises is also done once a week.

How do they rev the engine? "Our kids do some sort of strides every day," says Coach Joan Hunter. The team incorporates strides as part of their dynamic warm-up routine. They will also do 8–10 x 20 seconds at mile pace followed by 8–10 x 100m strides before big workouts. Not far from their school, they do hill strides or hill sprints as part of their easy runs. For example, they might run 8 x 10 seconds fast uphill with a downhill walk recovery, or do 6–8 x 20 seconds, starting at mile pace and speeding up with each repetition, finishing the last set at 800m pace.

At least twice a week, if not more, Loudon Valley uses wickets, or mini-hurdles, to improve running mechanics and speed. Coach Joan Hunter arranges four sets of wickets so that all of her athletes can run through the set that's appropriately spaced for their individual abilities.

For logs, the team uses the Final Surge platform, which Coach Joan Hunter reads daily. She encourages her kids to see patterns in their training—when they feel good, when they feel slight fatigue, and so on. That helps her and the athletes better individualize the training.

A highlight of the year is the full-day relay. Athletes camp in the stadium for 24 hours. In teams of three or four, they run 1,600m legs over and over. Their parents have a cookout in the evening, and come back in the morning to serve breakfast.

American Fork Boys Team

> School: **American Fork High School**
>
> Town: **American Fork, Utah**
>
> Enrollment: **2,400**
>
> Team Composition: **Boys**
>
> Coach: **Timo Mostert**
>
> Team Size: **30 (cross country); 20 (outdoor track)**
>
> Classification: **6A (largest classification)**

What have they accomplished? Nine state cross country championships, four runner-up finishes. The team has made NXN nine times, finishing as runner-up three times. Individually, they've had a two-time NXN champion, Casey Clinger, and seven individual state cross country champions. They have the national record for the 4 x 1600m relay of 16:41.30 (with splits of 4:26, 4:08, 4:05, and 4:02).

How do they build the engine? A cornerstone of Coach Mostert's program is the capillary run, which his athletes do every seven to 10 days, including during the competitive season. This run is 70 to 90 minutes and run at aerobic threshold pace (6:00 to 7:00 per mile), with the goal of completing the

American Fork's 4x1600m national record holding relay splits: 4:26, 4:08, 4:05, and 4:02.

second half faster than the first. Several days a week, they also do an interme-diate run, which is six to eight miles, also run at aerobic threshold pace. Each Monday during the pre-season, they run the "Grinder," which is 8.5 to 10.5 miles with 1.3 of it uphill. Finally, in off-competition weeks, they incorporate "power runs" of two miles at a pace that's 30 seconds slower per mile than 3,200m race pace.

How do they strengthen the chassis? Each week, the American Fork boys are in the weight room on Monday, Wednesday, and Friday to do upper body lifting; Tuesday and Thursday, they do their "mega-abs" core routine. Monday through Friday, after morning recovery runs, they do 10 pull-ups, 20 dips, and 40 crunches.

How do they rev the engine? Before every speed workout, they do seven "pull-outs," which are gradually faster strides of about 50m. With these, they focus on form. At least once a week, they run two "stride-laps," where they jog the turns and gradually accelerate to a full sprint on the straights.

Coach Mostert focuses on building the aerobic engine as the first priority of his program. For speed workouts, his athletes do longer repetitions—800m, 1,000m, 1,200m, and 1,600m—while trying to run negative splits. They do as much work on grass as possible.

The athletes each have a mileage log that starts at the beginning of summer training, and they are expected to keep it updated throughout the year. On Memorial Day and Labor Day, Coach Mostert collects the logs and even publishes them on the team's blog. Awards are given based on the records the athletes keep. Each summer, athletes aim to run 750 miles, or an average of 60 miles a week.

In July, the team has a three-day camp, where they run, discuss training philosophies, and nutrition, as well as enjoy games, campfires, and Dutch oven dinners.

Each summer, athletes aim to run 750 miles, or 60 miles a week.

St. Joseph–Ogden Girls and Boys Team

Pauline

Ogden

Glover

Saint Joseph

State Road

Tipton

School: **St. Joseph–Ogden High School**

Town: **St. Joseph, Illinois**

Enrollment: **450 students**

Team Composition: **Combined**

Coaches: **Jason Retz**

Team Size: **20 girls and 15 boys (cross country);
15 girls and 10 boys (outdoor track)**

Classification: **1A (smallest classification)**

What have they accomplished? The girls have won three cross country state championships, and the boys have finished as high as third at the state meet. Between the cross country and track programs, they have earned 18 team trophies and 459 all-state medals.

How do they build the engine? Throughout the year, they run a weekly long run that is anywhere from 60 to 90 minutes. The last 20 minutes of the run is "up tempo," making this faster than an easy run. They also do threshold work, increasing the duration throughout the year and always finishing knowing they could have done more. Younger athletes may get in 20 minutes of work at threshold pace, while older athletes may get in as many as 40 minutes. Athletes have input as to what type of workouts they'll do, with Coach Retz assigning fartleks and "broken tempo" options, where he adjusts the pace and rest to meet individual needs.

How do they strengthen the chassis? Three or four times a week, the athletes do hurdle-mobility drills, SAM routines, and sand walks to strengthen their hips and glutes. Coach Retz encourages his athletes to take a strength-training class, offered by the school as a physical education class, which means that most athletes lift four days a week. With Olympic-style lifting, they focus on improving their range of motion. "We want the chassis to be able to handle any load and any amount of horsepower," Coach Retz says. He also has his athletes incorporate rope stretching, foam rolling, and fascial-release techniques: "We don't stretch to gain flexibility. We stretch to find areas of soreness or tenderness. This lets us identify things we can do to help the area or identify possible changes to work-out plans that will keep them stay fit and healthy."

How do they rev the engine? After most recovery runs, the athletes run strides. They may go 100m, building up to 90 percent. These are often done barefoot. The other type of stride is a version of a flying 40, where the athletes hit full race speed and hold it for 40m. This ends up being about 100m: 30m to accelerate, 40m at full race speed, and 30m to decelerate.

Every day, the runners do some form of ancillary work—speed drills, wicket runs, or timed flying 10m and 40m sprints, which they do in spikes. They also have simple plyometric and hopping drills throughout the week.

Athletes are required to keep logs, which Coach Retz and the full roster can view on the team's website. There are rewards in the program for every 1,000 miles. If an athlete logs 6,000 miles, they earn a plaque at the school's annual awards night. "Logs help athletes reflect on their daily performances," Coach Retz explains. "They help them become more self-aware of the work they are putting in alongside their teammates."

A team camp each summer lays the foundation for their cross country season. They discuss goals, learn foundational principles of the program, and "become a family." Each week during the season, they have team meals, where they can enjoy each other's company outside of practice.

"We want the chassis to be able to handle any load and any amount of horsepower."

Minster Girls Team

New Bremen

Minster

Lehmkuhl La

Earls Island

S

Fort Loramie

School: **Minster High School**

Town: **Minster, Ohio**

Team Composition: **Girls**

Coach: **Jessie Magoto**

Enrollment: **280**

Team Size: **25 (cross country); 10 (outdoor track)**

Classification: **Division III (smallest classification)**

What have they accomplished? Thirteen state cross country titles and six runner-up finishes. Three state meet records: most wins, lowest score, and largest margin of victory. Thirteen track and field state titles. Alum Sunni Olding finished tenth as a junior and fifth as a senior at the Footlocker Championships.

How do they build the engine? A key element in Coach Magoto's training is the weekly long run, specifically progression long runs at an easy pace—but that finish faster. Athletes are talking easily at the start, but as the pace quickens, they're only able to talk in short phrases. By the end, they're running "fun-fast," which Coach Magoto describes as "not going 100 percent, but getting after it." This workout can vary from five to 10 miles, and is based on ability and strength rather than age.

They'll also run 5-minute repeats on a rolling grassy loop that is 1,000m.

A key element in Coach Magoto's training is the weekly progression long run.

For these, they take a 3-minute recovery, and aim to get faster as the workout progresses. Coach Magoto uses this loop, in part, because it helps her athletes focus for 5 minutes—without worrying about hitting a specific time for a set distance. They simply try to go a little farther each repetition.

How do they strengthen the chassis? The team goes to the weight room for everything from squats and hang cleans, to bench press and incline press. During the summer, they gather three times a week for hour-long sessions; during the season, they head to the gym twice a week for 20 minutes. "My distance girls are not afraid of the weight room," Coach Magoto says, "and not afraid to put real weight on the bar." Before an athlete adds a new lift to her training schedule, she first learns proper technique from the school's football coach. The team also does a hurdle-mobility and mini-band routine two to three times a week, while rope stretching helps improve lower-body mobility and flexibility.

How do they rev the engine? At the end of both long runs and recovery runs, the girls do strides. Prior to workouts, they do drills and strides.

Coach Magoto also asks athletes to swim and play water polo as part of their training, whether or not they have a background as a competitive swimmer.

Each athlete logs her times, recovery, and reactions to workouts using paper and pencil.

Gratitude is an important element of Coach Magoto's program, and the girls share the things they're grateful for on "Thankful Thursdays."

"My distance girls are not afraid of the weight room, and not afraid to put real weight on the bar."

Mountain Vista Boys and Girls Team

School: **Mountain Vista High School**

Town: **Highlands Ranch, Colorado**

Team Composition: **Combined**

Coach: **Jonathan Dalby**

Enrollment: **2,300**

Team Size: **55 girls and 55 boys (cross country);**
35 girls and 35 boys (outdoor track)

Classification: **5A (largest classification)**

What have the boys accomplished? Have won the NXR Southwest region twice, and have qualified for NXN four times, finishing third in 2017.

What have the girls accomplished? Have won the NXR Southwest race twice, and qualified for NXN three times, finishing sixth in 2017.

The team has swept all six races—varsity, junior varsity, and open, for both girls and boys—six times at the Continental League cross country championships.

How do they build the engine? Coach Dalby's athletes complete a long run, between 40 and 90 minutes, every seven to 10 days in the summer and winter. Sometimes they'll run 6–8 x 30-second surges during the second half of the run; other times, they may do a 10-minute "pick up" at the end. During the track season, the frequency of the long run decreases to every 12 to 15 days, and it is often replaced with 15 to 25 minutes of threshold running.

Coach Dalby uses "rhythm runs," which are essentially slower tempo runs for five to six miles. Sometimes athletes will do a 20- to 25-minute tempo run; sometimes they'll do a "broken tempo," running 2 x 10 minutes with a 2-minute recovery jog. They also incorporate faster than tempo pace, roughly aiming for 10k pace: 6–7 x 1,000m with a 200m recovery jog, for example.

How do they strengthen the chassis? Most days the athletes start with dynamic mobility work. They take this seriously, spending as much as 15 minutes on it before they run. Athletes hit the weight room two to three times a week, though this depends on its availability (as it's shared with other sports). Challenging lifts like hex-bar deadlifts and goblet squats, as well as simple exercises like pull-ups and lunges, are done during these sessions, which can last between 20 and 25 minutes. The team typically does hurdle-mobility work twice a week.

How do they rev the engine? "We run lots of hills," says Coach Dalby. The team refers to the system of hills behind the school as the "playground," and they view this work as a great way to build muscular strength when they can't get into the weight room. They'll often do 10-second hill sprints

The athletes take dynamic mobility work seriously, spending as much as 15 minutes on it before most runs.

rather than strides, doing as many as 10 and walking back to the start for their recovery. In the winter, when the track is iced over, they might do 10 x 30-second hills, with 3 to 4 minutes of walking recovery. Why the walk? Coach Dalby wants fast repetitions at a high intensity, and the generous recovery helps achieve that.

Coach Dalby preaches "sleep, hydration, and nutrition." He explains, "There are lots of ways to design training and workouts that will benefit athletes, but if you don't take care of recovery, the workouts won't help at all." He uses the phrase "the other 22 hours of the day" to help his athletes focus on this reality.

Training logs are optional at Mountain Vista, though athletes must keep one from Memorial Day to Labor Day if they want an "Aerobic Monster" shirt at the end of the summer.

Each year, athletes set goals as part of the annual team barbecue, and they take a team-building trip at a nearby state park. Because any Mountain Vista athlete can make the trip to the NXR meet, provided they work hard and contribute to the team's success, as many as 60 athletes might compete.

Sandburg
Boys
Team

School: **Sandburg High School**

Town: **Orland Park, Illinois**

Team Composition: **Boys**

Coach: **John O'Malley**

Enrollment: **2,900**

Team Size: **50 (cross country); 45 (outdoor track)**

Classification: **3A (largest classification)**

What have they accomplished? State cross country champions in 2015 and fourth at NXN. Two Footlocker Individual Champions. The average 4 x 800m time over the past decade is 7:44.4 (this includes setting the Illinois state record of 7:37.3). Five different athletes have run 4:10.1 or better for the 1,600m.

How do they build the engine? Athletes typically do a long run once a week, working up to 90 to 95 minutes. Once they are comfortable with that duration, they shift to progression long runs. "High-end aerobic work is always present," Coach O'Malley explains. "This includes building lactate threshold, progression runs, and controlled intervals."

How do they strengthen the chassis? Rather than do static stretching, athletes do strength and mobility work every day; this sometimes includes

Five different Sandburg High boys have run 4:10.1 or better for the 1,600m.

hurdle-mobility exercises. They spend a lot of time working on movement patterns, which help improve muscle recruitment. Athletes go to the weight room, though they limit their time to 15 to 20 minutes and focus on running-specific movements. The young men also have medicine-ball and mini-band routines they can do outside or at home.

How do they rev the engine? Coach O'Malley often says, "Our feet are moving fast every day." He uses everything from sprints up short, steep hills to maximum-velocity sprinting. The team does strides—anywhere between 50m to 200m—at approximately mile effort, with the focus on improving mechanics. "Strides are a basic example of my 'feet moving fast' principle," he explains. "We want to engage, recruit, and stimulate fast movement patterns, better range of motion, and muscle groups that often go dormant or are under stimulated while running slowly." Runners also use plyometrics, box jumps, speed-agility ladders, and wickets throughout the season.

Athletes are not required to keep a training log; Coach O'Malley measures overall training stress rather than keep detailed notes on mileage.

The Sandburg program emphasizes the empowerment of each athlete. "Each day, every runner is expected to have an answer for the following: How are you making yourself better today? How are you making the team better today?" The answer might be a psychological, emotional, physical, or other contribution to the team.

"Our feet are moving fast every day. We want to engage, recruit, and stimulate fast movement patterns."

Great Oak Girls and Boys Team

School: Great Oak High School

Town: Temecula, California

Team Composition: Combined

Coach: Doug Soles

Enrollment: 3,200

**Team Size: 60 girls and 90 boys (cross country);
50 girls and 70 boys (outdoor track)**

Classification: Division I (largest classification)

What have the boys accomplished? The NXN title in 2015 and three top-three finishes. Times of 7:35.06 in the 4 x 800m relay (a 1:53.8 average) and 16:52.95 in the 4 x 1,600m relay (a 4:13 average).

What have the girls accomplished? Three top-three NXN finishes. Times of 9:03.31 in the 4 x 800m (2:15.8 average) and 19:52.88 in the 4 x 1,600m (4:58 average).

Fourteen state cross country championships and six top-three NXN placings between the two squads.

How do they build the engine? Coach Soles believes "the best way to build a distance runner is through long runs," so his athletes do one (and sometimes

Daily, athletes do 4 x 60m sprints, form drills and speed ladders. This helps develop "controlled, balanced runners."

two) each week during the cross country season. Other key workouts include 5 x 1,000m and tempo runs of four to six miles. Several times throughout the week, athletes run twice a day. A "double" may include four miles in the morning and a fartlek session in the afternoon. Coach Sole also schedules HIITs—high-intensity interval training—three times a week.

How do they strengthen the chassis? Five days a week, athletes spend 30 to 50 minutes on core strength, choosing from over a half-dozen routines. They also do medicine ball routines and plyometrics, or a HIIT segment. Outside of practice, athletes are encouraged to do as much "prehab" as possible.

How do they rev the engine? As part of their daily warm up, athletes run 4 x 60m sprints and do form drills and speed ladders. This helps young athletes, in particular, develop into "strong, controlled, balanced runners." Quick turnover is also a priority: "We do something fast each day in our program," Coach Sole says, "whether it is a HIIT, sprints, or intervals." His team will often finish workouts with 2–4 x 150m, to end the day with fast running. And during the cross country season, they run hill sprints every Monday.

Because Nike Cross Nationals is often run in difficult conditions, Coach Soles has adapted his training accordingly. Every two weeks, roughly, his athletes run a workout in a sandy ravine—either 5 x 600m or 4 x 800m—giving them confidence they can race well on a muddy course.

Some athletes keep a training log, but they're not mandatory.

Great Oak "families" consist of four athletes—a junior or senior girl and boy, and a freshman or sophomore girl and boy. Older athletes answer questions and help younger athletes on race day with their warm ups. They also cheer them on at the finish of their races. During "Color Wars," the entire program is split into three: red, white, and blue teams compete throughout the week, which culminates with a freshman-sophomore one-mile race, with the older athletes serving as coaches.

"The best way to build a distance runner is through long runs."

Get Started Today

We're at the end of the book, which means it's time to start. It's time to start implementing elements from the previous pages so that you can become an excellent runner. It's time to start with a basic question: Knowing what you know now, what is the one thing you can do today to become a better runner?

Committing to daily chassis-building work is the first choice for many athletes (you can't go wrong with that one). Perhaps revving the engine most days is missing from your training. If that's the case, it's time to get moving. Now that you know how important sleep is for the growing high school athlete, maybe you can hone this aspect of your daily life, starting tonight. Eating enough food and having the word "nutritious" describe much of that food is crucial for your running success, and this may be the piece of the puzzle that helps you race at a higher level. These are just a few examples of things you can start working on this week or even today.

We've covered several keys to unlocking your potential that are long-term processes or approaches to your training. Running by feel is one of the few skills you need to learn as a runner. The sooner you embrace this concept, the better your chances of staying on top of your training—and being ready to race well at all of the important meets. Younger runners need to know that they'll be uncomfortable in races, while older runners need to have the courage to tell their coach about a niggle before it leads to an injury. Every runner on the team is going to have a better season if they're finishing workouts knowing they could have run farther or faster (or both). By no means are workouts going to be easy. Older athletes may only be able to say "a little farther" or "a little faster." The key is that if you embrace this concept, you give yourself a better chance of stringing together more days of injury-free training, which leads to faster racing.

After reading the case studies, you know there are dozens of ways to train. You also know that engine building, chassis strengthening, and engine revving are always present in winning programs (in some form or another). Most runners—regardless of age and experience—struggle with the reality that progress is not linear. You'll no doubt make jumps in performance if you follow your coach's lead. It's also important to love the sport enough that if you do hit a plateau, you're not discouraged.

You know now that talent and excellence are not the same thing, and that your goal is twofold: to become an excellent runner in high school and to become a lifelong runner. Multiple times each week, you can move toward excellence by building your attention span for hard work. This may come in the form of staying mentally engaged on a long run or checking that you're running with

Knowing what you know now, what is the one thing you can do today to become a better runner?

good posture. Other days, it may mean staying focused during the chassis-building work—which typically comes at the end of a training session when you're both physically and mentally fatigued, or thinking about the schoolwork that awaits you at home. If you want to race fast, if you want to transcend a former self and run a PR, building your capacity for hard work is essential.

The final point I want to make in this book is a simple one.

To start, choose just one thing to work on rather than several. Then work on it consistently, knowing that most of these suggestions can't be done every day. If you choose to improve your sleep habits, that's fantastic! Know that you'll need to be kind to yourself if you're only getting four or five nights of championship sleep at the beginning. Similarly, not every athlete will have chassis-building work assigned 365 days a year. The goal is to simply do the work when your coach assigns it, so that the word "consistency" applies. And when you feel that first concept has become second nature, incorporate another one.

In the introduction to this book, I said, "If your goal is to run progressively faster at the end of each season, then consistency is the key." It's really that simple. So where will *you* start?

So
where
will you
start?

Resources

Throughout the book, I referenced a number of useful resources that you can find at CoachJayJohnson.com/CIKbook. (If you have your phone handy, you can simply point your camera at the QR code on the next page.) If you're ready to take your training and racing to the next level, you'll want to take some time and explore the following resources.

Training Videos: I've created a library of routines that you can (and should) do before you run. I've also put together a number of chassis-building routines you can do afterwards. You've read that "simple ain't easy," and this quote captures the work you'll find here: simple routines that are challenging. I'll be adding to this library periodically, so make sure you join my email list to be notified when new clips are added.

Helpful Documents: You know that revving the engine is important, yet you may not know how to write a progression for doing strides. Don't worry: I've got a progression written for you! That's the kind of helpful document you can find. Other documents include information on nutrition, sleep hygiene, and visualization. And if exercise physiology is your thing, I've included detailed articles about how it can inform intelligent training.

186

Camps and Courses: I've been fortunate to be a camp director for close to 20 years, and I would love to meet you for some summer training. Camps don't work with everyone's schedule, and that's why I offer online courses that go deeper into the concepts we've covered in this book. If you're passionate about the sport and willing to do all of the little things to be an excellent runner, you're the type of student who will likely enjoy the courses, which you can do on your own timeline.

Finally, I'm @coachjayjohnson on social media. My Instagram content is mostly geared toward high school runners, while my Twitter account is essentially for coaches. Give me a follow!

Acknowledgments

When I told my friend and fellow coach Jeff Boele that I wanted to write a book for high school runners, and that I needed an editor who knew running on a deep level, he told me to talk to Kyle Wyatt. Kyle coached me through this process, taking my awkward drafts and helping me shape them into an accessible book. I'm forever indebted to him for his tireless work. Throughout this process, Kyle was training hard, chasing his dream of running the best race of his life at the 2020 U.S. Olympic Marathon Trails. He did just that. The 235th seed going into the race, he finished 101st.

I've known Adam Batliner for well over two decades, and he was the only person I wanted to design these pages. We ran hundreds of miles together in college, and we've had adventures backpacking in Colorado and exploring slot canyons in Arizona. (I should also note that he ran in the most exciting high school race I've ever seen.) Working together on a book was a new adventure. He understood what I wanted from our first conversation, then went about the magical process of transforming a manuscript into an engaging layout. Thank you, Adam.

I've been blessed with a long string of coaches, from my elementary school days through college, who spent hours and hours helping me learn to love training and competition. I appreciate all of you, particularly Mark Wetmore. My teammates at the University of Colorado showed me how to work harder than I could have imagined. They taught me how to trust the process, and how to run my best on the most important days of the year. I'm grateful for those lessons.

As a young college coach, I overcame my shy nature and asked coaches who I respected a lot of questions. Mike Smith, coaching at rival Kansas State, answered dozens of questions and, in the process, became a lifelong friend.

I've never met a coach I respect who doesn't occasionally say something to the effect of "I wish I could go back and work with so-and-so, because they would run so much faster given what I know now." To all of the athletes I've been blessed to work with, thank you for trusting me with your training when I was still learning the craft of coaching. I hope you'll forgive all of my errors.

I firmly believe that high school runners are the soul of our sport. And what's unique about high school distance coaches is their willingness to selflessly share what they know. I'm grateful that each of the coaches profiled in this book agreed to share insights into their programs—just another example of distance coaches helping athletes they'll never work with.

Numerous people took time to read this book in its early stages. Thanks to each of you for the feedback, especially Laura Sturges, Alex Lyons, and Whitney Macon.